GLOBAL HISTORY OF THE PRESENT
Series editor | Nicholas Guyatt

In the Global History of the Present series, historians address the upheavals in world history since 1989, as we have lurched from the Cold War to the War on Terror. Each book considers the unique story of an individual country or region, refuting grandiose claims of 'the end of history', and linking local narratives to international developments.

Lively and accessible, these books are ideal introductions to the contemporary politics and history of a diverse range of countries. By bringing a historical perspective to recent debates and events, from democracy and terrorism to nationalism and globalization, the series challenges assumptions about the past and the present.

Published

Thabit A. J. Abdullah, *Dictatorship, Imperialism and Chaos: Iraq since 1989*

Timothy Cheek, *Living with Freedom: China since 1989*

Alexander Dawson, *First World Dreams: Mexico since 1989*

Padraic Kenney, *The Burdens of Freedom: Eastern Europe since 1989*

Stephen Lovell, *Destination in Doubt: Russia since 1989*

Forthcoming

Alejandra Bronfman, *On the Move: The Caribbean since 1989*

James D. Le Sueur, *Between Terror and Democracy: Algeria since 1989*

Mark LeVine, *Impossible Peace: Israel/Palestine since 1989*

Hyung Gu Lynn, *Bipolar Orders: The Two Koreas since 1989*

Nivedita Menon and Aditya Nigam, *Power and Contestation: India since 1989*

Helena Pohlandt-McCormick, *What Have We Done? South Africa since 1989*

Nicholas Guyatt is assistant professor of history at Simon Fraser University in Canada.

About the author

Stephen Lovell is reader in modern European history at King's College, London. He is the author of *The Russian Reading Revolution: Print Culture in the Soviet and Post-Soviet Eras* (2000) and the prize-winning *Summerfolk: A History of the Dacha, 1710–2000* (2003). He has written widely on topics in Russian social and cultural history.

Destination in Doubt: Russia since 1989

Stephen Lovell

Fernwood Publishing
NOVA SCOTIA

Zed Books
LONDON | NEW YORK

Destination in Doubt: Russia since 1989 was first published in 2006

Published in Canada by Fernwood Publishing Ltd, 32 Oceanvista Lane,
Site 2A, Box 5, Black Point, Nova Scotia B0J 1B0

<www.fernwoodbooks.ca>

Published in the rest of the world by Zed Books Ltd, 7 Cynthia Street, London
N1 9JF, UK and Room 400, 175 Fifth Avenue, New York, NY 10010, USA

<www.zedbooks.co.uk>

Copyright © Stephen Lovell, 2006

The right of Stephen Lovell to be identified as the author of this work has
been asserted by him in accordance with the Copyright, Designs and Patents
Act, 1988.

Cover designed by Andrew Corbett
Set in Arnhem and Futura Bold by Ewan Smith, London
Index: <ed.emery@britishlibrary.net>
Printed and bound in Malta by Gutenberg Press Ltd

Distributed in the USA exclusively by Palgrave Macmillan, a division of
St Martin's Press, LLC, 175 Fifth Avenue, New York, NY 10010.

A catalogue record for this book is available from the British Library.
US CIP data are available from the Library of Congress.

Library and Archives Canada Cataloguing in Publication:
Lovell, Stephen, 1972-
    Destination in doubt : Russia since 1989 / Stephen Lovell.
Includes bibliographical references and index.
ISBN 1-55266-203-9
    Russia (Federation)--History--1991-. 2. Soviet Union--History--1985-1991.
I. Title.
DK510.76.L69 2006   947.086   C2006-902636-X

ISBN   1 84277 664 9 | 978 1 84277 664 3 hb
ISBN   1 84277 665 7 | 978 1 84277 665 0 pb

Contents

Acknowledgments

I am especially grateful to Nick Guyatt, the series editor, for his invitation to write this book and his inspiring contributions at various stages of its preparation.

Several people have helped me enormously by commenting on chapters: for this I thank Emma Gilligan, Alena Ledeneva, Elizabeth Teague, Vera Tolz, Federico Varese, and Tom de Waal. Barbara Heldt, Geoffrey Hosking, and Gerry Smith did me the great service of reading the entire manuscript in draft. For the first time in my life I feel bound to set down the conventional disclaimer: none of these readers, all of them more knowledgeable than I in their respective fields, bears any responsibility for errors of fact or eccentricities of interpretation that have sneaked into the final text.

I also thank Liz Leach for telling me that I should do the book and checking my metaphors.

My other great debt is to the Leverhulme Trust, whose award of a Philip Leverhulme Prize gave me the time to complete the manuscript.

Introduction

I arrived for my first and last extended stay in the Soviet Union in September 1991. At the time I would not have said that this state was about to collapse. Most of the people I encountered were in favor of maintaining the union, and a referendum held in March of that year had seemed to spell out the same message. The idea of viewing the Soviet experience as a bygone era would have struck many people, me included, as bizarre. The boom in historical publications during the late 1980s had if anything revived a general sense that Lenin and Stalin, Revolution and Great Terror, were still part of the present. As I moved in with the family to which I had been assigned in the medium-sized city of Yaroslavl, just over 150 miles northeast of Moscow, I was greeted with an anti-Western diatribe from the household's staunchly Stalinist babushka. Her outbursts repeated themselves throughout my stay, though they were somehow good-natured and I never needed to take them personally. This elderly woman, born less than a year before the October Revolution, had entered the industrial workforce, along with millions of others, in the 1930s. She had then worked for decades in a factory that boasted of manufacturing the world's first ever synthetic rubber tire; everything that she had experienced in her life had made her a proletarian patriot of the USSR.

In 1991, then, it was still counterintuitive to view the Soviet Union as a purely historical phenomenon. Even stranger would have been the notion that, within fifteen years or so, one might speak of the period *after* the Soviet Union in historical terms. Yet that is precisely what I am trying to do in this book.

Would-be historians of post-communist Russia have at least one practical thing in their favor: an abundance of sources. Readers seeking material on Russia in the 1990s are already spoilt for choice. In a very few years, Russia went from information drought to information glut. In the first half of the 1990s, Russian journalists were unrestricted, outspoken, and incisive to an extent that had no precedent in Russian history and few precedents elsewhere. Major political figures wrote memoirs with unseemly haste. Even purportedly fictional accounts teemed with insights into the financial shenanigans of the new elite or the violent machinations of the criminal underworld.

Many publications were spectacularly unguarded. In December 1999, for example, a national newspaper published transcripts of phone conversations between the populist television presenter Sergei Dorenko and the tycoon Boris Berezovsky in which the two men discussed in gleeful detail how they would scupper the election chances of Moscow boss Yuri Luzhkov. In the West, revelations of this kind would end the career of a TV presenter and seriously embarrass the tycoon. In the event, however, neither man was greatly inconvenienced: Berezovsky cheerfully vouched for the authenticity of the tapes, and carried on regardless.

The sheer volume of available material – not all of it reliable, of course, but much of it fascinating and informative in one way or another – makes the most recent period of history a bracing change for Russia-watchers whose formative experiences occurred in the Soviet era. As well as minute-to-minute journalism and more or less self-interested insider memoirs they can draw on a number of excellent books by foreign correspondents posted to Moscow for half a decade or more. They also have at their disposal a mass of sociological research on household budgets, public opinion, and so on. Most European societies that have been at the stage of introducing free elections or capitalist institutions have not come under anything like the same empirical scrutiny as Russia in the 1990s. Imagine, for example, that researchers in Imperial Germany or Third Republic France had conducted monthly public opinion surveys of representative samples of the electorates in these societies. Or consider what paths European democracy might have taken if the first mass elections in these political systems had been televised.

Last but by no means least, we can draw on the contribution made by scholars. Although the so-called Sovietologists took a great deal of verbal punishment (much of it unfair) for failing to foresee the imminent collapse of the system they devoted their careers to studying, they did not lose heart and redirected their efforts toward making sense of Russia's complicated and fragmented move away from state socialism. As they did so, they were able to join forces with two intellectual camps from which they had been regrettably separated for decades. First, they had the company of social and political scientists whose background was not necessarily in Russian studies. Second, and if anything more important, they could work in tandem with Russian researchers. As I have surveyed the scholarly output on contemporary Russia, I have found it hard to avoid the pleasant conclusion that plenty of bright and industrious people have been drawn to the study of post-socialism.

In this book I hope to give some sense of what they found to intrigue them. I will also try to explain where Russia belongs in a global history of the present – or, more bluntly, why Russia (still) matters. The very fact of posing this question indicates how much has changed in the last fifteen years. The place of Russia in the global picture now requires special pleading in a way it absolutely would not have done back in 1989. When Gorbachev was presiding over the dismemberment of the Eastern bloc, he was at the very heart of events. Since then, Russia has ceased to be the "evil empire" and become instead the (very) poor relation of the prosperous West. As the perceived power of Russia has decreased, so has its glamor. The goose-stepping soldiers outside Lenin's Mausoleum no longer inspire so much as a frisson of intimidation. The Bolshoi Theater, far from offering crack troops for the cultural front, has come to seem tawdry and stodgy by turns. University enrollments for Russian studies programs are down on both sides of the Atlantic. Even Tolstoy and Dostoevsky no longer seem quite so worth reading when Russians are seen to be not uniquely soulful but deprived and tasteless. Russian sports results have mostly been appalling since 1991; especially in team sports such as soccer and ice hockey, the decline has been precipitous. Even chess, physics, and classical music, the last bastions of Russia's Cold War cultural supremacy, have been weakened by emigration and the collapse of state funding. Not only are Russians less interesting to us now, there are also many fewer of them. The demographic decline that became perceptible even in officially published Soviet statistics from the 1970s onward has now become a crisis. And the rise of AIDS and drug addiction has led to comments that post-Soviet Russia has taken on the worst of the West while failing to assimilate the best.

Yet Russia remains important and fascinating in post-Soviet times, for all kinds of reasons. It brings into sharp focus the meanings and limitations of democracy. It highlights the problems of economic and demographic transformation in a largely obsolescent late industrial society. It can also offer insights into nationalism, nation-building, and decolonization.

Russians, moreover, find themselves at the sharp end of security issues that are by no means only "their problem." We are often told that we now live in a "post-9/11 world," and that we must all change our attitudes and behavior to take account of the American sense of trauma and outrage. That is undoubtedly true: partly because the Americans have reason to be shocked and angry, and also because the rest of us have no choice but to take seriously their government's reaction. But it is worth remembering that certain other parts of the world had fewer illusions before the Twin Towers fell. Before September 11, 2001, in many parts of the West, wars were things that other people got into thousands of miles away. In Russia they happened on ordinary people's doorsteps. In the late Gorbachev era, when the Soviet system began to unravel, the war of annihilation waged by Nazi Germany on Soviet soil was still alive and painful in the consciousness of Russian society. Worse still, the Nazis had recently been joined by historical demons closer to home. The violence perpetrated on Soviet society by its own ruling party had never been, and would never again be, so prominent in public discourse as it became in 1988–90, as the media made ever more shocking disclosures about the killing fields and subterranean firing squads of the Stalin era.

But state violence as a real day-to-day threat had thankfully become remote for most Russians. The post-Stalin leadership, after a moderate amount of bloodletting in 1953, had made sure there would be no recurrence of terror. The regime remained repressive and thought nothing of flouting human rights, but it did not routinely engage in the extra-judicial killing of its own citizens. Wars with Soviet participation were fought, but not on Soviet soil. Violence was still a recent enough memory for Soviet people that many were grateful for its absence and dreaded its return.

Unfortunately, however, the return of violence is one of the stories that has to be told about post-Soviet Russia. It is true that some of it was a matter of perception as well as reality. The contract killings and turf wars of organized crime affected a relatively small section of the population but gained disproportionate prominence in mass media that were overcompensating for the removal of Soviet taboos on the reporting of bad news. It is also the case that violence failed to ignite in some of the potential flashpoints of Soviet decolonization. But there is a limit to the good news. In December 1994, the Russian Federation launched a bloody and disastrous war with the renegade republic of Chechnya. Not only did this conflict send tens of thousands of civilians and conscripts to their deaths, it also did much to unleash on Russia's major cities the force of modern terrorism. Nor was Chechnya the only security problem on the territory of the Russian Federation or in its immediate vicinity. In October 2001, at a time when the Western media were fixated on the start of the bombing campaign in Afghanistan, I remember the invasion being placed as no more than fourth or fifth item on Russian TV news: more pressing issues included security problems in Georgia, Uzbekistan, and Chechnya, and the disappearance of a Russian passenger plane over the Black Sea (this disaster, which cost nearly 100 lives, turned out to be the result of wayward fire by Ukrainian forces out on military exercises). Russian defense experts, interviewed at length for their insights into the global terrorism alert, took a longer and more detached view than many of their Western counterparts. They were inclined to doubt that the Americans had the experience or the expertise to deal effectively with the terrorist threat. The hard-won wisdom of Russia's security analysts was that effective penetration of terrorist networks was the only effective means of struggling with thinly spread but resilient resistance movements.

All this is not to say that the Russians are especially to be admired. It is one of the most besetting Russian national myths that suffering equals virtue. It is also clearly untrue that Russia has found adequate – not to mention morally acceptable – ways of dealing with its unruly neighbors: one of the bitter ironies of the Yeltsin era was that the administration apparently took so little notice of the intelligence expertise at its disposal when reacting to its own crisis situations. All I wish to say is that America, far from being unique in its vulnerability to threats to "homeland security," is in fact a global second-ranker.

Another reason to write a history of Russia in recent years has less to do with global factors. It is simply that we need to ask ourselves more searching questions about what has gone on since 1989 or 1991. It is probably time to stop using the phrase "post-Soviet era" as if it somehow explains something about how post-1991 Russia is different from what came before. We need to apply those traditional historian's questions – of continuity and change – to the 1991 break, as well as to the decade and a half that has followed it.

Of course, it is not true that commentators have relied blandly on the concept of the "post-Soviet" era. In their efforts to construct an analytical framework, many of them have deployed a more ambitious term: transition. The resulting new field of research, "transitology," was one of the few growth industries in Russia in the first half of the 1990s. It represented a laudable attempt to impose intellectual order on enormously complex events, but it also had inbuilt limitations. Emphasizing transferable social-science techniques over local knowledge, it often proceeded from the unspoken assumption that Russia must, if it were to avoid disaster, transform itself into a version of America, Britain, or Germany. It also presupposed that the USSR was usefully comparable with other regions of the world that were parting company with dictatorship, even if their political structures and social conditions were very different from those in the Soviet case.

This is not to say that the search for comparative material is fruitless. An enormous number of analogies have been proposed, all of them illuminating in one way or another. A representative but far from exhaustive list would include Pinochet's Chile, sixteenth-century England, post-Risorgimento Italy, the antebellum United States, late tsarist Russia, the Holy Roman Empire, Weimar Germany, Guatemala, Mozambique, and Paraguay.

The metaphor of "transition" seems useful and appropriate if we retain its connotations of departure and movement but hold back from assuming that a predetermined destination named "liberal democracy" has already popped up on the horizon. History must, in my view, involve some awareness of contingency – a sense that things might not have turned out the way they did. For this reason, one has to be suspicious of accounts that treat the Soviet collapse as "inevitable" or the Soviet system as "unreformable." The point has by now been endlessly belabored, but it is still worth recalling how few people in the mid-1980s predicted the Soviet Union's imminent demise.

It is also important to keep in mind the bewildering number of options that seemed open at various stages of political change. In April 1988, right-thinking people worried that a Stalinist article by a Leningrad schoolteacher named Nina Andreeva might signal the derailing of reform. Authoritarian revanche seemed constantly to be in the air – until the atmosphere cleared somewhat after the botched coup of August 1991. Once the Soviet state had been dismantled so unceremoniously at the end of 1991, many commentators stopped looking backward to Soviet repression and switched to regarding Russia as a blank slate. In some respects they were not wrong. Any account of post-communist Russia must be considered a failure if it does not give a sense of the speed and scale of change in 1990–92. Most fundamentally of all, the fall of communism marked the end not just of seventy-odd years of state socialism but of five centuries where the strengthening of the state had been of paramount importance. Back in the thirteenth and fourteenth centuries, the Mongols taught Russia's rulers a lesson they did not forget: given the size and openness of the Eurasian land mass, a strong centralized state was imperative for survival. What this implied was a patrimonial regime where a strong ruler handed out dominions to servitors, rewarding them but also making them responsible for extracting resources from the population. This mode of governance was probably the best way of exploiting and galvanizing a country that was large, poor, thinly populated, and vulnerable to attack. Needless to say, it did not do much for human rights, democracy, and the rule of law.[1]

According to this interpretation of Russian history, the Soviet era can be seen merely as the latest variation on a long-standing theme. This was what the brutal, patrimonial, highly centralized

Russian state became in response to the new challenges thrown up by modernity. Urbanization and industrialization were essential to keep pace with European great powers that all seemed predatory to the Bolsheviks. The Soviet regime sought its own ways to avoid the social and political problems that tended to accompany modernization in the West: it built a new kind of national pride, it stood for some kind of social justice, and (most obviously and importantly) it pushed the coercive powers of the modern state much further than liberal democracies wished, or were able, to do.

And then, all of a sudden, in 1991, the mighty Russian/Soviet state signed itself out of existence. Russia moved from saggy totalitarianism to a rustbelt state of nature in a matter of months. The Soviet Communist Party was abolished on Russian soil. Soviet institutions were disbanded in a tearing hurry. Although analogous institutions did appear at the level of the new Russian Federation, they proved ineffectual in many areas. The Russian state was bad at collecting taxes and even worse at performing its redistributive responsibilities. It could not create the conditions for economic stability by securing the currency against inflation. Worse still, it was unable to underwrite the rule of law and lost its monopoly on violence.

At the same time, the government was granting its people an unprecedented degree of freedom. Journalists could print whatever they wanted, and citizens could read whatever they could get hold of. The state no longer controlled pricing, and trade was liberalized. People could travel freely and work where they chose. Last but probably not least, Russian citizens aged eighteen and over were allowed to vote in elections whose outcome was at least some of the time in doubt.

As our historical perspective on the emergence of a new Russia has begun to lengthen, all-encompassing theories of social and political change have come to seem rather less adequate and interesting. A useful clue is given by scholarly usage, which has begun to prefer words like "transformation" and even "revolution" to "transition." Revolutions are eternally fascinating to historians because they represent moments when all the most fundamental rules of political and social interaction are subject to challenge, where the direction and outcome of change are wholly unclear, and where decisions made by key actors under enormous pressure can have extraordinarily far-reaching consequences. They strip life down before our eyes to naked realities of power, belief, solidarity, and survival that mostly remain hidden from view in complex modern societies.

This is why I think that post-Soviet Russia deserves the attention even of people who have no special interest in this part of the world. Russia's transformation raises so many of the big questions about how human beings operate: what democracy means and how it works; how private property rights can be justified and enforced when they have hardly existed hitherto; how people can part with money without receiving their return on it immediately in person. Most of these questions are far from our minds as we go about our daily business in the UK or the USA, and a very good thing too. I sincerely hope that few if any of the readers of this book will have seen their life's savings wiped out in a few days or weeks, or their country signed out of existence by a cabal of politicians, or their national industries privatized in rigged auctions, or their leaders cheerfully exposing themselves as massively corrupt and/or incompetent. (Some Western leaders may in fact be incompetent and corrupt, but they at least make more effort to conceal the fact than did the ailing Boris Yeltsin and his cronies.) Such things became almost routine in Russia in the 1990s – not to mention genuinely everyday phenomena such as malfunctioning or non-existent public services, delays of several months in payment of state pensions and salaries, and the extortion of bribes by office holders. As more than one commentator has pointed out, if there is one word that can characterize post-Soviet Russia, it is uncertainty.

Perhaps, in this light, the problems and crises of the first post-Soviet decade are only to be expected. What requires explanation is how, in spite of all these troubles, Russia has gone on functioning. We need to ask, in the words of one perceptive recent study, "how Russia really works."[2] We need to put firmly to the back of our minds one of Winston Churchill's more unfortunate *bons mots*: the notion that Russia is a riddle wrapped in a mystery inside an enigma. To be sure, much that goes on in contemporary Russia is alien or antithetical to Anglo-Saxon notions of statecraft or economic rationality, but that does not relieve us of the task of making sense of it. Quite the opposite, in fact.

One final preliminary word. This is a short book with little space for blow-by-blow accounts, biographical vignettes, or dense empirical detail (however fascinating and important all these things might be). There are already many excellent books on post-Soviet Russia where readers will find much fuller analysis than can be provided here: I have been able to acknowledge at least a few of them in the "Guide to Further Reading."

Given the space constraints I have chosen what I hope will seem a straightforward layout for the book. Each chapter seeks to answer a question that an intelligent Western onlooker might ask of contemporary Russia. These questions, needless to say, have all spawned debate and controversy, especially among experts. They have no simple answers, but they can at least be simply stated:

1 What was the socialist legacy for post-Soviet Russia?
2 How strong is Russia, and does it constitute a threat either to its own citizens or to the wider world?
3 Is Russia democratic?
4 What is Russia, and who are the Russians?
5 Does Russia have a free market?
6 How have post-socialist Russians got by on their pitiful salaries and pensions?
7 Is Russia involved in a global "War on Terror"?

1 | What was Soviet socialism?

Let's start with a rarely asked but vital question: What were the values that came closest to holding together the citizens of the Soviet Union on the eve of that state's collapse? After all, a state does not remain in existence for seventy years and become a superpower without creating some sense of commonality toward which members of society can gravitate.

If we are looking for sources of unity in the late Soviet period, however, we should not expect to find anything so narrowly ideological as Marxism-Leninism. To be sure, every Soviet schoolchild was forced to learn the most celebrated dicta of the communist founding fathers. Leninist slogans were invoked everywhere in public life. Even quite independent-minded authors of works on recondite subjects such as medieval history or Renaissance sculpture would find themselves throwing in a couple of quotations from Lenin's *Collected Works* as a sop to the censors or their editorial committee. But I never met anyone in Soviet Russia who had any real interest in Marxism, and I met plenty who despised it. As everyone knows from their own brushes with boredom, the human brain develops defense mechanisms against the invasive repetition of dogma. "Ordinary" people tend just to switch off, while intellectuals react more feistily. Anti-Marxism is the closest thing to an orthodoxy that I have found in the academic circles of Moscow and St. Petersburg. As one Russian colleague asked me a few years ago, "Why are you all [i.e. Western Slavists] such lefties?" Post-communist Eastern Europeans, in my experience, are hugely suspicious of anything that smacks of state interventionism: they view political correctness with disbelief and have difficulty comprehending the soft totalitarianism of the audit culture.

What, then, are we left with? Were there any commonly held values that emerged from the Soviet experience? I think there were, and I would group them in three main categories. First came a cluster of beliefs that were broadly socialist: an expectation of a strong redistributive state and some notion of social justice. Of course, opinion varied – from one era to another, and from one individual to another – about who exactly should be the beneficiaries of the state's redistributive largess. In the postwar decades the categories of beneficiary became more numerous and more elaborate, as more and more groups of Soviet citizens gained a sense of entitlement to housing, vacations, pensions, and so on. Some Sovietologists went so far as to speak of the "social contract" of the Brezhnev era. In general, however, there remained some clear differences between Soviet and Western social democratic notions of entitlement: for the Soviets, usefulness to the state tended to trump human or natural rights as a criterion for social provision.

The second value that underpinned Soviet socialism as an active worldview was patriotism: the sense that the USSR was a great world power, that it had achieved great things (whatever crimes its leaders had perpetrated in the process), that it had saved Europe from the catastrophe of Nazism. World War II, for all the colossal collective trauma that it brought, may well have kept Soviet socialism in business as a belief system for longer than it would otherwise have warranted.

The third key value was a commitment to the various forms of social and economic progress that can be termed modernization: mass education (especially tertiary), urban development, science and technology, large-scale industrialization, the increased production of goods other than the basic necessities.

However, for all that we can identify elements of a positive belief system, it is hard to escape the conclusion that the best way to characterize the official face of Soviet socialism is in terms of what it claimed not to be. It was hostile to market activity and its associated phenomena: large inequalities of wealth, great accumulation of property in private hands, unearned income, profiteering, exploitation of one person by another. It also rejected what it presented as meretricious Western mass culture. As far as Soviet public discourse was concerned, culture was a sacred and elevated sphere of human activity that should not be contaminated by the profit motive. A further enduring pet hate of Soviet socialism was democracy in the Western liberal understanding of that term. Elections, or so said Soviet received wisdom, could not be free if they were ruled by the checkbook and if voters were duped by cigar-puffing media tycoons. Liberal democracy was bad because it was ruled by capital and did not produce rational government.

The Soviet Union, then, was on a mission to show the viability, and superiority, of an alternative route through modernity. It was to match and surpass the West in terms of measurable progress – industrial output, numbers in higher education, standard of living – but it was also to avoid the pathologies of advanced capitalism.

By the end of the 1970s these claims were ringing very hollow indeed. The Soviet Union was clearly not becoming prosperous. Soviet patriotism was no longer as robust as it once had been. The war generation was growing old and dying, and national groups that had fewer reasons to look back fondly at the victory of 1945 (Estonians, Lithuanians, Latvians, Chechens, Ukrainians) were becoming more politically assertive. Soviet socialism, if observed at close quarters rather than in an ideological haze, contained many gray areas. Unlimited private property was bad, but some degree of individual property was legitimate. Constructive criticism of the system and its failings was healthy, but it was not to shade into dissent. The West was the benchmark in many economic and technological matters, but how to accept this while continuing to uphold the distinctiveness and superiority of the Soviet way of life?

By the middle of the Brezhnev era, it appears, many people were overstepping the line between critical reflection and disloyalty. A small minority did so by consciously rejecting the principles and practices on which the Soviet system was based. These dissenters – the kind of people who might have read George Orwell's *Nineteen Eighty-Four* or Solzhenitsyn's *First Circle* ten or fifteen years before these works were finally published in the USSR – knew all too well that Soviet socialism was a profoundly flawed and morally compromised system of social and political organization. Such people, who mostly did not carry their opposition into the realm of public action, may well have numbered a couple of million in the late Soviet period.

Millions more, however, showed their independence from the tenets of Soviet power in more mundane ways. Perhaps they told jokes about their increasingly senescent leaders. Perhaps they were privately skeptical of the foreign news coverage they saw on their televisions or read in their newspapers. Perhaps they coveted a Western tape recorder or leather jacket, or yearned to take a holiday in France. Such people also belied the rhetoric of socialism in more tangible ways. They regularly redirected state property toward the second economy, they stole time from the state by taking three-hour lunch breaks and moonlighting, and they used personal contacts to improve their access to collective goods such as education and healthcare.

Examples like this suggest that it is not adequate to speak of Soviet socialism merely as a belief system (even if we accept that the beliefs were not strictly Marxist-Leninist). Socialism was also a civilization or, more simply, a way of life. One of the basic facts underlying this way of life was the absence of political pluralism. Although the coercive powers of the state were used less drastically in the post-Stalin era, they were still considerable. Under these circumstances, to express radical disagreement with state policy was an act of heroism, not a viable option for the vast majority of the population. This did not mean, however, that people were all, or even mostly, "true believers." They might well engage in the notorious Soviet activity of "doublethink": saying one thing in public and quite another in private, but without perceiving this as inconsistency or hypocrisy.

Another basic fact about Soviet socialism was that money was not as significant as in Western liberal democracies. Inequalities of earnings were much lower, and most people could not hope to amass large sums in their bank accounts. Even if they did, money on its own could not buy many of the things that people most wanted: a flat in Moscow, a car, a foreign trip. Soviet society was not radically egalitarian: it was structured by inflexible hierarchies of status. But such hierarchies were not expressed in the same way as in the USA or even France or Germany. They were not reflected in conspicuous consumption but rather in regular privileged access to goods that were supposed to be collectively owned.

There were two main ways of ensuring such access, and they

were complementary. One was to work for an organization that was in a strong position to lobby for a greater than average portion of collective resources. The other was to know the right people – or, at least, to make the best of those people one did know.

Money was relatively unimportant not just in people's everyday lives but also at the higher levels of economic management. As the Hungarian economist János Kornai has notably argued, Soviet enterprises enjoyed "soft budget constraints." That is, they knew that in most cases the state would bail them out if they failed to balance their books. They also had strong incentives to maximize their own access to scarce resources (such as raw materials) instead of converting those resources into goods for resale. For these reasons, hoarding and ad hoc bargaining were endemic in the Soviet "planned" economy.[1]

The opacity of economic relationships may be taken as symptomatic of a closed society where nothing of fundamental importance was ever exposed to free public scrutiny. Soviet society had its "winners" and "losers" – its privileged elite and its permanently poor – but such disparities could never be publicly discussed, though they were common knowledge among the population. Governance in the Soviet Union depended on a mighty apparatus of rule that formed a rigid pyramid from Moscow down to the village soviet. Yet the practical operations of this system were more fluid and personalistic than its bureaucratic forms might suggest. At every level of authority, office-holders were accountable not to the population at large but to their immediate superiors in the hierarchy of the party-state; their power depended partly on those superiors, but also on the network of informal relationships they were able to strike up with people of approximately equal status in their own locality: directors of collective farms, newspaper editors, industrial managers. This was not a system that could be eliminated, or even fundamentally transformed, merely by abolishing the Communist Party.

All in all, the diagnosis for the USSR circa 1989 cannot be considered a favorable one. In Ken Jowitt's trenchant words, its undesirable characteristics included:

a "ghetto" political culture that views the governmental and political realm suspiciously, as a source of trouble, even of danger; a distrustful society habituated to hoarding information, goods, and goodwill, which shares them only with intimates and is filled with Hobbesian competition; rumor as a mode of discourse that works against sober public discussion of issues; a segmentary, not complementary, socio-economic division of labor in which the semi-autakic workplace favors social insulation; a political leadership whose charismatic-storming approach to problems did very little culturally or psychologically to familiarize these societies with "methodically rational" action; and Soviet-enforced isolation between the nations of Eastern Europe, something that reinforced and added to their mutual ignorance, distrust, and disdain.[2]

To this imposing list of attributes I would add a basic social and political conservatism. Soviet citizens valued stability and order in a way that perhaps cannot be fully comprehended by members of prosperous societies that have never (or not recently) experienced revolution, world war or state-sponsored terror on their own territory. But this does not affect Jowitt's conclusion that very little in 1989 seemed to predispose Russia to liberal capitalist democracy.

The rest of this book will explore how Russia moved on from this highly unpromising situation. I do not think I am spilling too many beans if I say that the story will not always be a pretty one. But it is also important not to be cynical or fatalistic. The tendency in most historical writing is to argue that the Soviet system, with all its stresses and internal contradictions, was created in the 1930s, and then to wait for the clock to tick down on it. In this reading of Russian history people are denied much in the way of choice and agency. In 1991 they were plunged into a state of near-anarchy where only the luckiest and the most unscrupulous could prosper. The fact is, however, that systems decline not only because it is their internal logic to do so but also because particular people at particular times take particular decisions. The Soviet political system would not have collapsed if Gorbachev had not exposed the party-state to contested elections. And, once it had collapsed, the possible outcomes seemed extraordinarily, and worryingly, indeterminate and open to contestation. With the aim of recapturing at least some of this sense of uncertainty, the chapters to come will run the clock forward from 1989.

2 | The state: death and rebirth?

All history is comparative history. Whether we admit it or not, when we write an account of a particular country or individual we have other such accounts in mind. At the very least, this other material suggests to us what matters are worthy of discussion: how much time, for example, a biographer should spend on the subject's school days or marriage or published writings. Often, however, the insights we draw from comparison are more fundamental. We measure the person or political culture we are investigating by the standards set by other people or cultures.

For the last three hundred years or so, Russia has persistently, even obsessively, measured itself by reference to a part of the world called "the West" or "Europe." Partly, no doubt, this preoccupation has been a matter of geopolitical necessity: Russia's rulers had to take care that other great powers did not take liberties. But "the West" was an object of fascination mostly for the lessons it could give, or the warnings it could serve, to intellectuals and policymakers concerned with Russia's internal development. Russia was lagging behind in cultural, economic, social, and political terms. The crucial question was what exactly it could learn from those parts of the world that were ahead of it. How should it incorporate its tens of millions of enserfed peasants into a dynamic modern economy? How should it run its schools and universities? How fast should it industrialize? How radically should it look to change its political institutions?

Western Russia-watchers may have differed from Russian observers in the answers they provided to these questions, but their frame of reference was similar. Russia was backward in all kinds of ways, and an assessment of its future depended on its prospects of overcoming this predicament. The intensity with which Russia and the West were compared only increased in the second half of the twentieth century. In the Cold War, the Soviets and the Americans sized each other up in all kinds of ways: they compared military arsenals, political systems, economic performance, standard of living, city planning, sports teams, musicians, and so on. No area of human existence was so mundane that it could not engage the competitive instincts of the superpowers. In 1959, Nixon and Khrushchev faced off over a kitchen sink at the American exhibit in Moscow as they argued over the relative merits of domestic interiors in their respective countries.

The USSR came off significantly worse from this proclivity to compare. To say this is not simply to benefit from hindsight. When Khrushchev declared that the Soviet Union would catch up and overtake the West within a matter of years, he did not hear the Americans make a reciprocal boast. Even as brash a Soviet patriot as Khrushchev took it as axiomatic that Russia still had some catching up to do.

Russian history looks rather different, however, if you put it in a truly global context. The image of "the West" held by generations of Russian intellectuals from the early nineteenth century onward overlapped with empirical reality in very few parts of Europe: Britain, in some ways France, in other ways Germany. It did not bear much resemblance to Spain or Italy or Austria. Russia's tendency to measure itself by this gold standard of progress and civilization reflected ideals more than achievable aspirations. Perhaps a more valid and meaningful point of reference would be Turkey: another precarious empire, reactionary polity, and backward economy that was not able to enter the twentieth century with much confidence.

Russia appears in a different light if, instead of condemning it to the outer reaches of the developed world, we place it in the vanguard of the Third World. It seems to meet many of the relevant criteria. In the early twentieth century it was poor and economically underdeveloped. It was prone to corruption, authoritarian government, and political strife (revolution, civil war, mass terror). But it also served as an example to the many other similarly afflicted parts of the world by finding a drastic response to its predicament. It industrialized at breakneck speed, in the process exterminating millions of people (mainly peasants) who appeared to stand in the way. It launched a mostly successful mass education campaign:

illiteracy was all but liquidated and a new elite of managers and professionals was trained. Perhaps its most significant achievement, however, was that it built and consolidated a strong state.

States are things that people in the West tend to take for granted. Yet clearly we would be floundering if we did not have anyone to run our armies, oversee our education systems, maintain our roads, implement our laws, and punish our criminals. We would also probably feel unsettled if we did not belong to a nation (however strong our other allegiances, such as religion or region, might be), and nations almost always need states to back them up. The price we pay for all this is to allow the state to collect our taxes and to enforce laws that may sometimes inconvenience us. All things considered, however, this seems a price worth paying, as the alternative – to organize all these things ourselves – would be hugely time-consuming, stressful, and (almost certainly) more inequitable than the arrangement we currently have.

The advantages of the state are even more obvious if we take the vantage point of those people with ambitions to govern a society. If there is no functioning army or bureaucracy, even the wisest policies and laws are likely to be worth little more than the paper on which they are written. Under these circumstances, government may well slide into corruption and warlordism.

Yet, if we take a global and historical view, strong and stable states are the exception, not the rule. Even in the twentieth century, there were plenty of rulers and governing elites who had no effective long-term means of controlling and managing their societies. The kind of concentration of authority and power that a strong state requires does not happen automatically. If anything, quite the opposite: the single most favorable precondition for creating a strong state is massive social dislocation. In a revolution or a civil war, existing structures of authority – monarch, court, plutocracy, aristocracy, colonial power – are swept away. Society is polarized in a life-or-death struggle for power. The effect of this is to consolidate hitherto fragmented political forces: peasants and proletarians, for example, may previously have had very little in common, but in a revolution they may find themselves on the same side and sign up to the same political agenda (even if they understand it in different ways). When their side comes out on top, state-builders have a mandate more powerful than any they could have acquired in less cataclysmic circumstances.

The analytical framework I have been presenting owes much to Joel S. Migdal's study of Third World state-building in the postwar era.[1] But it works rather well for Russia too: if ever there was a case when a centralized and tyrannical state emerged from revolutionary strife, and in the face of military threats from abroad, Bolshevik Russia was it. Not only did the Soviet Union consolidate its statehood earlier than the nations that emerged from postwar decolonization, it also proved much stronger and more enduring than most of them. Its strength seems to have been directly proportional to the exceptional violence that attended its creation.

Migdal's concern was less to analyze the circumstances under which Third World states are formed than to explore the ways they operate in practice. He showed that, once such states come into being, their effectiveness is seriously compromised by the carrot and stick methods that their ruling elites are forced to employ. The position of these elites is not sufficiently secure that they can afford to ignore the power bases established in key areas by other groups – industrial managers, for example, or regional bosses. What results is a "pathological style at the apex of the state": leading officials, who might otherwise help the state to achieve its objectives, are eliminated because they constitute a threat to the elite's monopoly of power. Conversely, for all the stern rhetoric of the political elite, this elite is forced to reach a working arrangement with interest groups in the state apparatus if it wishes to get anything done. Regional "strongmen," their local bureaucrats, and the central state authorities thus often form a "triangle of accommodation."

We could apply Migdal's insights to the Russian case as follows. In the first half of the Soviet period, the state was very tough with potential pockets of autonomy in the apparatus (witness Stalin's purges). As time went on, however, it abandoned mass terror as a personnel management strategy and cut more deals with local elites. Some of these deals involved outright corruption and circumvention of normal procedure. But they were more likely to entail giving promising loyal and youngish party functionaries their head. Much is made of the "gerontocracy" of the Brezhnev period, and that is certainly a valid description of the Politburo in the 1970s and early 1980s. But at the next rung down the political hierarchy – at the level of provincial party secretary – we find if anything a rejuvenation of personnel. Mikhail Gorbachev was part of a generation of upwardly mobile bright young things.

By the start of the 1980s this political system seemed as well entrenched as at any time in the Soviet period. It no longer needed violence in order to police itself. It had stable means of reproducing itself through the cultivation and eventual promotion of junior "cadres." And, of course, it remained in possession of a formidable apparatus of social control: the KGB, the Communist Party, the army (to name only the most important institutions).

The problem, however, was that the apparent monolithic unity of the system concealed an increasing diversity of opinion within the elite. A number of fissures had opened up within the broad ruling class along generational, ideological, and ethnic lines. Brezhnev's policy of greater accommodation with regional branches of Soviet power had made party bosses in national republics, including Russia itself, more politically assertive. Newish members of the elite did not have Stalinist industrialization or the Great Patriotic War as their formative experiences: their adulthood or early maturity was more likely to have been colored by de-Stalinization or Prague 1968. Worse still, it was becoming clear that the Soviet economy was underperforming. The envisaged solution, as always, was to mobilize the Soviet people to work harder and better. But how exactly to achieve this, given that violence on the Stalinist scale was no longer an option and ideological exhortations on their own had little chance of success? An increasing number of younger members of the *apparat* believed that the solution was to borrow at least a few elements of the more open, less market-averse, socialism to be found in places like Sweden and the Netherlands. But their views were far from being universally shared in the Party.

These divisions, which were perceptible only to skilled Kremlinologists in the late 1970s and early 1980s, were brought into the open by the initiatives of Mikhail Gorbachev. To begin with, Gorbachev's actions were fully in line with Soviet traditions of ideological mobilization: he spoke in vague terms about activating the "human factor," he launched a crackdown on alcoholism and poor work discipline, and he urged a return to a purified Leninism. But in due course he undertook a series of more radical measures that had enormous implications for the future of the Soviet state. In the international arena he moved decisively toward arms reductions and distanced himself from the "Brezhnev doctrine" of unquestioned Soviet hegemony in Eastern Europe. Domestically, he resolved to encourage the Party to become more democratic – and to build institutions to that effect. Tensions within the Party were laid bare, and Soviet society was for the first time made privy to the cut-and-thrust of political debate. By the end of 1987, Gorbachev himself was made to look uncomfortable under these new conditions as he was challenged by an outspoken party boss from the provinces named Boris Yeltsin.

For the moment Gorbachev was in a position to swat away Yeltsin's challenge and force this firebrand into temporary retirement from politics. But he pressed on with political reforms that soon brought him even more trouble. In March 1989, deputies to a new Soviet assembly, the Congress of People's Deputies, were chosen by partially contested elections. At the end of May, the Congress proceeded to elect a full-time parliament, the Supreme Soviet. The following year, analogous parliaments were created at the level of individual Soviet republics, and the single-party monopoly was abandoned. Once permitted their own democratic political institutions, these republics quickly mutated into nations-in-waiting. Gorbachev greeted this predictable development with dismay, because he genuinely had not seen it coming: as a good Soviet patriot, nationalism was his greatest blind-spot.

But Gorbachev's most pressing political problem in 1990–91 was not nationalism in Estonia or Georgia but the rise of independent political institutions in Russia. The Russian Soviet Federative Socialist Republic (or RSFSR) had its first multi-party elections in the spring of 1990. The chairman of the new, Russian, Congress of People's Deputies, a certain Boris Yeltsin, was politically assertive from the start of his period in office. He declared Russian sovereignty and wasted no opportunity to claw power away from central

Soviet institutions, claiming that the RSFSR, not the USSR, had first claim on the civic obedience of its population. His hand was further strengthened when he was elected Russia's first president in June 1991.

Soviet Russia in 1990–91 thus found itself in a condition of dual sovereignty. Gorbachev and Yeltsin waged a "war of laws" where each man legislated to defy the authority of the other. Russians had no unambiguous answer to a simple question: What (or which) was the state? Most of them were in favor of Russian political autonomy, yet also wished to retain some kind of union. Both in public opinion and, more worryingly, in political circles it was unclear what exactly "sovereignty" meant, or how political jurisdictions might realistically be divided up between Russian and Soviet institutions. Here a great defect of the Soviet political system was exposed: pluralism was almost impossible to deal with. In a one-party state, political divisions could not be permitted to manifest themselves and persist: they had to be resolved by the *force majeure* of one or other of the contending factions.

It is not inconceivable, though rather unlikely, that the standoff between the USSR and the RSFSR could have been resolved by careful negotiation, and that the former could have remained in existence. In the event, the triumph of the latter was precipitated by a contingency: the failure of an attempt in August 1991 by Soviet hardliners to keep the USSR together by force. From this moment onward, the political momentum and legitimacy were all with Yeltsin, and the most fundamental question of all (whether a wholly independent Russian state should exist) was decided in the affirmative. After the defeat of this coup launched from within the Soviet system, Yeltsin wasted no time in claiming control of Soviet enterprises on Russian territory and in asserting the authority of the Russian government over Soviet ministries. On August 25, moreover, he took the momentous step of banning the Communist Party of the Soviet Union inside Russia and confiscating a large part of its property. In due course, he was able to acquire from the Soviet Union the key organs of security that Russia had not previously possessed: in November he issued a decree creating under his presidential control a set of Russian successor organizations to replace the Soviet KGB.

Yeltsin still had to resolve multiple questions of reciprocal obligations with other former Soviet republics – a particularly sore point
was control over the Black Sea fleet, which Russia disputed with
Ukraine – but now that a sovereign Russian state had come into
being, there was at least a solid political basis on which to seek
solutions to such difficulties.

A more intractable question at the end of 1991 was how this new
Russian state would actually function: how in practice power would
be exercised in the Russian Federation. The sudden removal of the
mighty ruling party had created a huge power vacuum. The organization that had controlled all appointments, run the military and the
security forces, allocated social benefits, and so on, disappeared at
a stroke. This had to be, and was, hugely destabilizing.

Though perhaps not quite as destabilizing as it might appear.
Although the Soviet state disintegrated, the people who ran that
state did not vanish into thin air. Mikhail Gorbachev was if anything
the exception: a man who had staked his political authority on the
Soviet state at an unfashionably late stage of its existence, and who
consequently lost just about everything in December 1991. Others,
who were more savvy or less principled (according to your taste), were
less compromised. A state, after all, is not just an idea in people's
heads: it is also made up of real people with a particular relationship
to each other, to the sources of political power, and to collective
resources. It was only to be expected that the new Russian state,
and Russian politics, were dominated by people who owed most of
their prominence to their previous careers as apparatchiks. Boris
Yeltsin was the shining example, but there were tens of thousands
of others, from Smolensk to Vladivostok, from the Congress of
People's Deputies to the administration of small towns in provincial
Russia. Communist office-holders did not find themselves radically
undermined in the way they did in other parts of Eastern Europe.
Even in 1995, only about one in six members of regional elites were
free of past association with the Soviet nomenklatura, and in the
president's inner circle the figure was only a little higher (just over
25 percent).[2]

Yeltsin may have steered clear of personnel purges partly out of
a determination not to repeat the destructive mistakes of the Soviet

past, but his main motivation was pragmatic. With old institutions and mechanisms of control collapsing around him, he desperately needed people with a shared institutional background and a common set of assumptions about how politics worked – and with some kind of effective power base even in the far-flung regions of the Russian Federation.

But to say that many of the same Soviet faces cropped up in the post-Soviet state does not on its own tell us much about what this state was able to accomplish. Quite apart from all the pressing practical problems of the handover from Soviet to Russian institutions, Yeltsin faced two fundamental structural issues. The first of them was the relationship between the executive (the president and his government) and the legislature (the Supreme Soviet, the working parliament whose members were drawn from the Congress of People's Deputies): these two institutions had emerged in a rush in 1990–91, when the energies of both were largely directed at challenging the hegemony of the USSR over Russia, but it was not clear how they would relate to one another in calmer times, when there was no unifying common enemy. The second issue was the relationship between the central government in Moscow and the regional governments in the eighty-nine territorial units ("subjects") that made up the Russian Federation. While the USSR had still existed, it was the "center," and Russia was one of fifteen elements in the socialist union. In the absence of the USSR, Russia was now itself the "center," and it was unclear how its various "peripheries" (twenty-one of them had the premier status of "republics," two were the "federal cities" of Moscow and St. Petersburg, while the rest were "provinces" [oblasts] and administrative "territories" [krais]) would respond: would they play by the center's rules, would they be obstructive, or might they even declare sovereignty in much the same way as Russia had recently done at the expense of the Soviet Union?

These were big questions that could have received at least the beginnings of an answer in the form of a new constitution. The last three months of 1991 were in many ways the best imaginable time to embark on building a new political order: Yeltsin's legitimacy was at an all-time high following his heroic resistance to the August coup, and old institutions were in such a state of upheaval that they were unlikely to put serious obstacles in the way of radical transformation. Yeltsin, however, decided to use his immense political capital not to redesign institutions but to tackle the economic problems that (not without cause) seemed to him more pressing at the time. This choice of priorities also reflected his deep political instincts. Yeltsin was a doer – an adept political tactician – rather than a thinker and a strategist. He canceled regional elections that were due to take place in December 1991 and chose not to hold national parliamentary elections to renew the membership of a Congress of People's Deputies that had been elected in a different state and a different era. He argued – not without some justification – that voting was a luxury the country literally could not afford at a time of economic crisis (though his instincts also told him that elections were not politically worthwhile, as they were not certain to deliver a more reform-friendly legislature). He postponed consideration of constitutional matters, and embarked instead on a program of radical reform using powers of decree that he had been granted for one year from November 1991.

This begged the question of what reform would entail. Yeltsin's political and economic program had been consistently vague up to this point – an excellent approach to take at a time of political instability, but not one that provided a firm foundation for statesmanship in the medium term. The vagueness of his policy statements had been matched only by the single-mindedness with which he fought Gorbachev. Some meaningful statements of intent did emerge from this politics of antagonism: where Gorbachev favored central power, Yeltsin wanted federalism; where Gorbachev wanted socialism with a human face, Yeltsin wanted a free market.

Market reforms were indeed Yeltsin's jumping-off point into post-communism, as was consistent with his populist problem-solving inclinations: the economy was undeniably the area of life that had the most painful direct impact on Russian society at that moment. But economic reform confronted Yeltsin with two political problems he had never faced as a charismatic party boss under the old system. First, this reform was bound to make things worse for the bulk of the population before it made them better. Second, Yeltsin was putting in charge people with no political base – a decision he would never have dreamed of taking in his earlier life as first party secretary in Sverdlovsk, and one that he almost never took even in the post-Soviet period (when he continued to rely heavily on patron–client networks he had established earlier in his career). The architects of reform – foremost among them the earnest, well-spoken Yegor Gaidar – were a group of (by Soviet standards) indecently young men who had emerged from research institutes, not from the Soviet *apparat*.

Yeltsin was undoubtedly reckoning on the fact that he could use the Gaidar team as fall-guys in the future, but he was also supremely confident in his own executive powers. He was counting on the continued support of the Supreme Soviet, the parliament that had served as his ally in the "war of laws" against the Soviet Union in 1990–91. The problem, however, was that the support of the parliament in this cause was not a blank check for future expenditure of political capital. An increasing number of deputies were dismayed by the direction economic reform was taking and began to express their opposition in intemperate and intransigent terms. They also resented the near-absolute powers the president seemed to believe that he possessed. As the Russian Communist Party grew in numbers, and as "democrats" (until now supporters of Yeltsin) began to defect to nationalist groupings, the Congress of People's Deputies turned against him. At the end of 1992, it struck a number of blows against Yeltsin, both failing to renew his powers of decree and forcing him to dispose of Gaidar.

The new year brought no resolution of the growing conflict. In the spring of 1993 Yeltsin tried to force through a referendum that would have invited the population to make a yes/no choice between president and parliament. In the end, after much wrangling, he ended up with a four-question referendum that gave him personally a vote of confidence (a 60 percent trust rating), expressed approval of the economic reforms (53 percent: apparently a modest result, but quite remarkable given the social costs of the reforms over the previous year), but also revealed a general impatience for parliamentary elections to be held sooner than scheduled. After this personal victory, however, Yeltsin still did not call new elections but rather set up an unelected "conference" to draw up a new constitution. This body soon lost any chance of maintaining the broad political base it needed: oppositionists declined to recognize its legitimacy, believing quite rightly that the president was trying to engineer a constitution to suit himself, and asserted the parliament's right to ratify a constitution of its own. On September 21, Yeltsin decreed the dissolution of the Congress of People's Deputies, and pressed on toward direct popular ratification of a new constitution.[3]

History perhaps has a habit of repeating itself, but it rarely does so as promptly as in Russia between the late summer of 1991 and the autumn of 1993. Just as in 1991 the conflict between the defenders of undiminished Soviet statehood and the upholders of Russian sovereignty reached an impasse where force was seen as the only solution, so in 1992–93 the presidential advocates of "reform" and of strong executive power locked horns with the defenders of parliamentarism. Once again Russia had dual sovereignty. On September 23, the Congress responded to Yeltsin's decree by appointing a president of their own, Aleksandr Rutskoi (hitherto Yeltsin's vice-president). Rutskoi headed a group of oppositional deputies who refused to quit the parliament building (the White House); Yeltsin turned the screw by cutting water and energy supplies to the building. Misjudging the level of active support they would be able to mobilize in Moscow and in the country as a whole, the parliamentary rebels issued a call to arms that led to attacks on the Moscow mayor's office and the Ostankino television station. At this point Yeltsin was in a position to take decisive retaliatory action. In a grim reversal of the events in August 1991, he sanctioned the shelling of the same building he had iconically defended two years earlier. The most striking difference between the two confrontations was the number of casualties: more than 100 dead in 1993, only three in 1991.

This tragedy had demoralizing effects on Russian political culture that will be analyzed for decades. In the short term, however, it enabled Yeltsin to force through the constitution he had neglected to have written for him at a more propitious moment in 1991. Unsurprisingly, this document gave the president strong leverage over a new lower house, the State Duma, whose powers were legislative and not supervisory. The upper house, the Federation Council, was made up of heads of regional elites (two from each of the eighty-nine "subjects of the federation") whom Yeltsin was confident of keeping on his side. The new constitution, aggressively promoted in the media, was approved by a referendum timed to coincide with the first post-Soviet parliamentary elections in order to ensure the required 50 percent turnout. Yeltsin duly gained 58 percent support for his constitution on a poor but adequate turnout of just under 55 percent (though both these figures were almost certainly inflated by fraud).[4]

Here, then, was the foundational document of the "Second Russian Republic" that came into being at the end of 1993. In the short term, it did not do anything to mollify parliament. The first Duma elections produced a 450-member assembly with a strong contingent of outspoken critics of the president, forty-eight of them from the Communist Party and sixty-four from the perversely named right-wing extremist Liberal Democratic Party. But, although vituperative exchanges abounded in the working life of the Duma, they did not subsequently bring the state to a standstill as they had done in 1993. The only drawback of the strong presidential system, from Yeltsin's point of view, was that it exposed the president every four years to ordeal by ballot box: if he were to fail, then someone else would reap the benefits of his constitutional powers. But, with the help of corruption and colossally biased media, Yeltsin passed the electoral test in summer 1996. In 1999, he passed on the presidential mantle to Vladimir Putin, who in 2000 and 2004 achieved election victories far more convincing than his patron's solitary success.

In other words, for the last dozen years Russia has enjoyed a stability of political system and a continuity of political regime that would have seemed enormously improbable in the middle of October 1993. The strong presidential constitution occasioned much parliamentary resentment in the second half of the 1990s, but it did not prevent a surprising degree of cooperation between president and Duma. The volume of legislation passed compared very favorably with other "cohabitational" systems.[5] Even more importantly, the Duma did not stand in the president's way when he twice took the most drastic measure at his disposal: the declaration of war (in 1994 and 1999, both times against Chechnya).

The paradox, in the light of all this, is that so many people, in Russia and outside, have bemoaned the weakness of the Russian state in the second half of the 1990s. The constitutional powers of the president did not seem to translate into unity of political purpose, still less into effective action. This purportedly strong state was not able to achieve much. Its revenue-generating capacity collapsed. It failed to maintain a stable economic environment. It presided over a disastrous collapse of morale and discipline in the armed forces and other security organs. Surveys in the late 1990s revealed that more than 80 percent of Russia's young men sought to avoid the draft. Official figures (which were almost certainly a gross understatement) revealed the desertion of 40,000 troops between 1994 and the first half of 1998.[6]

How to account for this string of failures? One problem lay right at the heart of government. The model of statecraft espoused by Boris Yeltsin, for all its modern presidential trappings, looked backward more than forward. He established the presidency as the executive equivalent of the Party in Soviet times: it loomed imposingly over the rest of government, and its apparatus soon became even more bloated than that of the CPSU. Not only was the presidential administration oversized, it was also understructured and militated against any efficient and transparent division of responsibilities and jurisdictions. In fact, inefficiency and opacity were themselves important techniques of governance for Yeltsin. Through the principle of "institutional redundancy" (that is to say, by ensuring that the functions of different agencies overlapped), he forestalled any effective challenge to his own authority.

As the Yeltsin era wore on, the anti-procedural proclivities of the president became more and more evident. He increasingly saw himself as a "people's tsar" and the patriarch of a political clan. He took to referring to himself in the third person. He stood above politics – in the sense of detailed policy formation – but also prevented his subordinates from carrying on coherent and concerted discussions in his absence. Rather, he played them off against each other, retaining for himself the role of ultimate arbiter of the fate of their policies and of their political careers. By the last two years of his reign, he was in the habit of firing ministers in ever more peremptory and self-exculpatory fashion. The effect of this arbitrariness was to increase the short-termism and self-interest of office-holders.[7]

The president's "clan" could also, of course, be a welcoming and protective place for those on the inside. Yeltsin had brought with him into the post-Soviet era not only his own trusted cadres but also the very principle that tight patron–client networks were the best way to extend control over the executive apparatus. Yet, as the criteria for power and influence shifted in the direction of "new money," these networks developed new points of entry. When people with independent clout – such as billionaire media moguls and owners of newly privatized major companies – found their way into the inner circle, they were almost impossible to dislodge, and completely unaccountable to anyone but the president himself. From 1995 onward, Yeltsin acquiesced in, and partly initiated, the complete interpenetration of political and economic elites: put simply, his method of governance made the Russian state massively and endemically corrupt.

But the dysfunctionality of the Russian state in the 1990s was not purely the result of Yeltsin's modus operandi. It also derived from the ground rules established by the 1993 constitution. The strong "superpresidential" system led to ad hoc particularist solutions. It did not work as a smooth organizational transmission belt whereby political decisions could be transferred into the realm of action. The inability of the court system to act as a check on the executive was a short-term advantage for the government but a medium- and long-term hindrance: the weakness of the law meant that decisions were unlikely to be properly enacted unless they were backed by a personal "enforcer." But this was an impossibly labor-intensive style of governance: the number of enforcers, their resources, and their attention spans were all limited, which ensured that the application of laws would be inconsistent and unfair – thus further undermining their credibility.

Given the unpromising signals from above, not much could be expected of the lower and outer reaches of the Russian state. Yeltsin was faced with the greatest challenge of governance in Russia – how to maintain any sort of effective control over regions as far as ten time-zones away – and he favored the solution adopted by many of his predecessors: to allow trusted plenipotentiaries fairly free rein in their own regions, on condition that they delivered their obligations (primarily taxes) to the center. Most of the time, these governors would be left free to maintain their local power base and to milk their position for personal gain, but occasionally they would be punished in order to remind them of their primary responsibilities to Moscow.

As practiced at other moments in Russian history, this system of governance was of course inefficient and inequitable, but it was less expensive to maintain than the short-term costs of moving to some other arrangement and it tended to meet the ruler's primary political needs: to maintain strong central power without relinquishing the enormous territories in the hinterland. Under Yeltsin, however, it worked rather differently, for two main reasons. First, the president did not have at his disposal the powers of coercion needed to underwrite this kind of autocratic decentralization – partly because of the weakening of his own faculties due to aging, alcoholism, and heart trouble, but also because the apparatus needed for such coercion had weakened drastically when the Soviet Union collapsed. Second, the eighty-nine "subjects of the federation" now had political and institutional instruments of insubordination to the center that the president himself had done a great deal to create. Back in the summer of 1990, newly minted as the Chairman of the Russian Congress of People's Deputies, Yeltsin had stormed off on a whirlwind tour of the Russian regions where he had famously urged local elites to take "as much autonomy as you can swallow." At the time, these declarations were yet another weapon in Yeltsin's struggle against the centralizer Gorbachev. But, when the national liberationist poacher turned into the state-building gamekeeper, his promises turned out to have stored up a lot of trouble. The years 1990–92 became known as the era of a "parade of sovereignties," as more than twenty territorial units of the RSFSR followed the lead of the union republics by asserting control over their own affairs (though, with the notable exception of Chechnya, they did not go so far as to proclaim full independence). Just about all of them started to lobby aggressively in Moscow and to view themselves as the negotiating partners of the center rather than obedient "subjects" obliged ultimately to bow to Moscow's will. In 1992, regional governments started to withhold taxes and to refuse to take part in the privatization campaign. The tug-of-war for resources between Moscow and the provinces, and between different parts of the provinces, was a permanent feature of post-Soviet politics.

Relations between center and periphery, like those between president and parliament, were hampered in 1992–93 by the fact that they were not on a firm constitutional footing. Unlike the president–parliament relationship, moreover, they never acquired such a footing in the Yeltsin era. Negotiations toward a new "Federation Treaty" had been underway since the summer of 1990, and in March 1992 this document was signed by all twenty-one republics in the Russian Federation except for Tatarstan and Chechnya. But it soon became clear that individual regions regarded provisions in the treaty not as binding but as negotiable. The voluble Bashkortostan demanded a bilateral treaty and was granted a special appendix of its own to the Federation Treaty. The remote mineral-rich republic of Sakha (formerly Yakutia) did not receive an appendix but was able to secure control over a sizable portion of its own precious metals and stones. These ad hoc arrangements, combined with the political weakness of a president busy doing battle with his national parliament, made provincial leaders disinclined to take the Federation Treaty seriously.[8]

In theory, Yeltsin's hand was much strengthened when he prevailed over his opponents in the White House in October 1993. Center–periphery relations were redrawn in Moscow's favor by the new constitution. In practice, however, discretionary arrangements continued to trump formal rules. Only weeks after the constitution was passed in December 1993, the Russian government signed its first bilateral treaty with a region (Tatarstan, the most recalcitrant of the federal subjects other than Chechnya). Bilateralism soon snowballed, to the extent that more than half of Russia's territorial units – not just the twenty-one republics, but many of the ordinary regions as well – had their own treaties by the end of the decade, and many of them were able to take the initiative in stipulating the special provisions that they required. Moreover, regional governments routinely flouted federal law: in 1997, the Ministry of Justice examined 44,000 regional pieces of legislation and discovered that nearly half were not in accordance with the Russian constitution.[9] Regional violations were regularly identified by the Constitutional Court but rarely corrected.

Why were the regions able to call so many of the shots against a central government that was, after all, capable of shelling its own parliament into submission? One important reason was that local elites were able to make meaningful the federal structures that had existed on paper in the USSR. While the party-state remained in power, federalism was a myth and regional elites took their orders from Moscow; the key institution was the local committee of the Communist Party, not the corresponding state body (known as the Soviet Executive Committee). In the last two years of the Soviet period, however, the CPSU lost its monopoly, the regions began to see open political contests for the first time, and members of the local soviet organizations were transformed from party stooges into "democratic" politicians (even if, in practice, they very often remained the same people with the same political instincts). Thus, when Yeltsin tried to argue with local elites in the 1990s, he was dealing not with the submissive clients he tended to recruit for his presidential administration in Moscow but with skilled and asser-tive political operators who had the benefit of a well-established institutional framework and enjoyed a democratic legitimacy in their own regions that was no less (and often greater) than Yeltsin's own. Many of them also had economic bargaining chips in the form of raw materials or industries that the federal budget could not afford to do without.

In this situation, the president could adopt one of two approaches in order to prevent the serious weakening of the Russian state: either he could assert direct central control over regional elites or he could attempt to co-opt them by slotting them into his political networks. In the event he tried both, but neither really worked. In his early burst of legislative activity in August 1991, Yeltsin created the position of presidential representative to oversee affairs in the regions, and he made several attempts during the 1990s to boost the authority of these appointees. But the resources at their disposal were always inadequate, their authority was undermined by ambiguity as to what their role really entailed, and their loyalties sometimes lay more with their allotted region than with their master in Moscow. They also became increasingly marginal as regional executives and legislatures began in the mid-1990s to follow a regular electoral cycle: presidential appointees had no obvious place in a provincial political culture where the keys to power lay not in Moscow but in the maneuvers of local elites and interest groups.

Yeltsin's main co-optation initiative was the creation of an upper house (the Federation Council) as part of the 1993 constitution. This body was made up of 178 delegates, two from each of the eighty-nine subjects of the federation. Yeltsin's intention was that, by giving these men status at the national level, the president would be able to turn them into his loyal enforcers in the regions. The real outcome was almost precisely the opposite. The Federation Council quickly developed an esprit de corps and provided an effective forum for regional elites to engage in special pleading and to defend each other's prerogatives.

But was the hemorrhaging of power from the center to the regions necessarily a bad thing? For regional elites, and for at least some of their constituents, it made a pleasant change from the Soviet practice of top-down directives. By the early twenty-first century, locally elected representatives enjoyed a great deal more popular support than their counterparts at the national level. The problem, however, was that the prevailing view of center–periphery relations as a zero-sum game was considerably less efficient and less equitable than a more cooperative strategy would have been. Its result was to reinforce already gross inequalities between rich regions and poor regions, between privileged and unprivileged sectors of the economy, and between rich and poor citizens. Not only did the weakness of Russian federalism serve to maintain inequality, it reduced Russia's economic adaptability in a critical phase. Besides reducing the capacity of the state to combat crime, it served actively to encourage corruption through the scope it allowed for particularism and special pleading.

By the late 1990s, then, the Russian state was underperforming disastrously in all kinds of ways. When Vladimir Putin came to power in 1999, he soon declared his intention to restore its strength. His first major set of legislation in May 2000 was designed to bring order to Russia's unruly federalism. He aimed to reinvigorate Yeltsin's system of presidential representatives. Dividing the whole of Russia into seven enormous "federal districts," he appointed a presidential plenipotentiary to each of them. Five of the seven appointees were generals, which left no room to doubt Putin's intention to bring a strong central executive hand to the fiefdoms of the regional governors. Drawing on his background in military and security organizations, he drafted army and KGB men into key positions elsewhere in the government. Unlike Yeltsin, Putin had the benefit of a sympathetic Duma and relied less heavily on regional governors to marshal votes for him in the presidential election. He therefore felt able to get tough with them. He declined to sign new bilateral treaties and to renew those that had expired. To much protest from incumbents, he removed the automatic membership in the Federation Council that regional executive and legislative heads had enjoyed since 1995. Declaring his intention to institute a "dictatorship of law" and to create a "unified legal space" in the Russian Federation, he announced a crackdown on republican or regional violations of the constitution. He also claimed the power to dismiss regional legislatures and executives in cases where serious violations were discovered.[10]

Statism quickly became the core value of the new presidency. Putin brought to the fore men from the military–industrial nexus of power who openly regretted the demise of the USSR. He also cracked down on a few of the people who, as he saw it, had done most to undermine the integrity of the state in the Yeltsin era (though he granted the greatest single culprit – Yeltsin himself – immunity from prosecution). Three of the business and media grandees of the 1990s – Boris Berezovsky, Vladimir Gusinsky, Mikhail Khodorkovsky – were forced into exile or jail.

Assertive Russian statism also had its usual corollary: a combative foreign policy. Putin was tough in negotiations with the EU and downright hostile in his treatment of Eastern European neighbors (notably Estonia and Ukraine). He sought solidarity with the USA after 9/11, but his support for US foreign policy was by no means unconditional. By 2005 he was deep in discussion with China and other members of a "Shanghai Cooperation Organization" whose immediate geopolitical goal was to curtail American involvement in Central Asia. But anti-Westernism, though it was clearly the ideological default setting for many in Putin's entourage, was not the overriding motivation of Russia's actions in the international arena. Robust pragmatism, rather, was its key element. Putin's first term went a long way to dispelling the reputation as a diplomatic loose cannon that Yeltsin had created through his eccentric summitry in the 1990s.

Enough has changed since 1999 for the Putin era to be widely seen as bringing an end to a decade of revolutionary upheaval and giving Russia back much of its self-respect. The president's admirers – and they are not few in his own country – might argue that he has done nothing less than create a model of Russian statehood revamped for the twenty-first century. To follow this interpretation in the direction of historical analogy, Putin is to Russia what Napoleon Bonaparte was to France: a man who owed his rise largely to the patronage he enjoyed under the *ancien régime* and then to the decisiveness he showed at a moment of revolutionary flux; who, despite uncharismatic appearance, developed a cult of personality; who restored patriotic pride to his country by building a strong centralized state; and who forced the other European great powers to take his country seriously just at the moment when they thought they could begin to write it off.

Putin is not about to embark on a Napoleonic campaign of conquest and expansion, but he does have a broad geopolitical vision. He sees Russia as a great power whose role is to exercise vigilant supervision over the "Near Abroad" of the former Soviet Union and to share the enormous Eurasian land mass with China as a sphere of influence. His overall mission is to defend his country against new threats that he sees emerging in a destabilized world order. With this end in view, he aspires not to replicate the political systems of other major states but to create something qualitatively different (and better): a state with a strong executive that is not hampered by parliamentary grandstanding or by needless legal niceties. Putin and his men view with perplexity and more than a hint of contempt the extended self-questioning that liberal democracies indulge in before extending the powers of the state to meet troubling new challenges (international crime, illegal migration, global terrorism). In their interpretation of history, liberal democracy became the norm in a small and privileged part of the globe for a brief moment in human history (the second half of the twentieth century), but now it is becoming obsolete. The USSR faced the worst of the twentieth century's horrors – revolution, civil war, famine, annihilationist "total war" – and never occupied the historical armchair seat from which liberalism may appear to be the destiny of mankind. Its main successor state, Russia, can thus form the vanguard of a new, pragmatic, stable, "modern," capitalist, non-totalitarian illiberalism; since 9/11 there have been gratifying signs that parts of the West may be ready to follow its lead. The "backward" great global powers of the twentieth century – notably Russia and China – may thus be about to show their "developed" postmodern counterparts the way to succeed in the twenty-first.

This is a highly speculative, though not altogether absurd, account of the direction in which the world is heading. I sketch it out here not to second-guess the future but to give some sense of the mindset of Russia's current rulers. Putin and his team are well acquainted with Western ways of life and systems of government, and find much to admire (especially in the economic domain), but they do not regard liberal democracy as the logical or even desirable end-point of history. Far from laboring under a sense of inferiority with respect to the West, they have a well-developed sense of their own worth.

How justified is the nascent superiority complex of Russia's rulers? Although it is still far too early to reach a firm judgment, there are already reasons to believe that Russia's state-strengthening program will fall short of the president's ambitions. The most substantial of them is that Putin has not quite created an effective new model of rulership but rather shows signs of reverting to a well-known Russian pattern: the over-controlling center. However tough Moscow tries to get, political actors in the provinces are usually adept at finding ways of pacifying the center while continuing to further their own interests. The bark of the presidential plenipotentiaries already appears to have been considerably worse than their bite. The central government's effective agency in the regions is thus limited, yet its figurehead, the president, by claiming responsibility for everything that happens in the country, raises expectations that he is bound to disappoint when he proves less than omniscient and omnipotent.

An even more fundamental problem is that, while the Russian state has started to be a little stronger in areas where it needs to be strong, it continues to be spasmodically strong in areas where it needs to be weak.[11] The law is no longer by any means an irrelevance in Russia, but it is still used as an instrument of rule with enough frequency that its potential role as impersonal arbiter of disputes is compromised. However authoritarian a state is in principle willing to become, it cannot intervene constantly to right perceived wrongs without exhausting its resources and its credibility: to work effectively, it has to permit more impersonal mechanisms (notably the law) to do more of the work.

In sum, although the institution of the strong president now seems well established in Russia, his capacity to act with decisive effect is still limited. Historians will debate for decades where exactly to draw the lines of periodization in the "Second Russian Revolution" of *c.* 1987 to *c.* 2000. As things currently stand, my guess is that, for all Putin's energetic efforts, the opportunities and limitations of Russian state-building were substantially determined by decisions taken, and not taken, between August 1991 and January 1992. In that honeymoon period of Russian independence, with vested interests as weak as they would ever be and political uncertainty at its height, Yeltsin's preference was to exercise power in the short term rather than to give it structure for the longer term, and this order of priorities has been replicated by the Russian ruling elite ever since. Individual political actors make an enormous difference at moments of revolutionary change, but their impact tends to decline thereafter, however loud their protestations to the contrary.

3 | Democratization?

One thing undoubtedly was new about the post-Soviet state: it was headed and run by politicians who endured trial by ballot box. After a hiatus in the first half of the 1990s, Russia began to meet several of the formal requirements of democracy. National elections – both legislative and executive – were held regularly. Yeltsin considered canceling the presidential contest of 1996 but was persuaded not to. Even Vladimir Putin, who is charged (or credited) with establishing a more authoritarian system of rule, operates not a plebiscitary dictatorship but a political system where the president, however great his constitutional powers, has to work with a parliament, stand for reelection after four years, and retire from office after two terms.

As well as being regular, elections were open, in so far as people were not disenfranchised for political reasons or barred from entering polling stations. Procedural violations did occur, but it seems that ballot papers were not torn up or miscounted on a scale sufficient to declare the electoral process meaningless. Although the Central Electoral Commission was by no means free of political influence and often put up arbitrary obstacles to the registration of parties, the main quantitative problem with Russian politics in the 1990s was that there were too many parties, not too few.

Regular, open and free elections are, however, only one of the criteria for effective democracy. A more important one is that elections should make a political difference: that these democratic appurtenances should enable members of society who do not hold political office to affect those who do. Political elites have two main ways of subverting the democratic process. The first is to set up a political system where election results do not matter much; where the government can carry on with minimal attention to the popular vote. The second is to change the way people vote using methods that go beyond legitimate political campaigning. In authoritarian societies this may be achieved through simple intimidation and repression, and by reducing civil rights – in particular the freedoms of speech and assembly. In non-authoritarian societies, politicians try to act on voters by changing what they think – or by making them imagine that the politicians think the same way as they do – and in their efforts to do so they may seek unfair anti-democratic advantages by, for example, blackmailing their opponents or paying journalists to give them favorable coverage.

Between 1986 and 1996, Russia moved from an authoritarian system where elections were held but made no political impact to a non-authoritarian system where elections mattered a good deal. But this was also a system spectacularly vulnerable to special interests. In all elections after 1991, the incumbent president enjoyed grossly unfair access to the media and free rein to blacken the names of his political opponents. Although he and his advisors did not always make best use of this advantage, they refined their techniques of televisual propaganda to such an extent that in 1996 they won an election that many sane and well-informed people had considered unwinnable.

Another criticism of post-Soviet political culture is even more fundamental. However much democracy comes to resemble show business in the West, there is supposed to be much more to it than the populist razzamatazz of national elections. In the four-year intervals between elections, democracy is much more to do with the daily cut-and-thrust, and give-and-take, of local politics. The major parties are not faceless national organizations represented solely by the platitudes and plastic handshakes of presidential or prime ministerial candidates. People in the West like to think that their democracies are nourished by "civil society": a wide range of organizations that spring up in the fertile middle ground between individual citizen and state.

On both these counts – party politics in the broad sense and civil society – Russia seemed sadly deficient. National parties were numerous but extremely weak in electoral terms and patchily represented at the local level. The tone was set by the most powerful man in the country, the president, who never felt it necessary or even desirable to acquire a party allegiance. Worse still, the Russian population did not seem desperately concerned by the democratic deficit of the post-communist era. Voters reelected a president (Yeltsin) who had been instrumental in dismantling their previous country and lowering their living standards. Opinion polls through the 1990s consistently showed that the word "democracy" elicited widespread skepticism. "Order" was a higher priority for most Russians, who later received their due with the "managed democracy" of the Putin era.

For many Western observers all this was a crushing disappointment. The Russian Federation was apparently propelled into existence by a wave of revolutions in Central and Eastern Europe, almost all of which resulted in more robust democracies than Russia's. For a brief period in the late 1980s and early 1990s, Russians seemed to be in the throes of a struggle with one-party dictatorship. Millions of people were politicized to a pitch of intensity that their already democratized counterparts in the West could never hope to attain: they followed political debates in their entirety, for hours on end, on their television sets; they read from cover to cover newspapers that retained the small print and long articles characteristic of Soviet journalism; they read highbrow journals and books that offered historical and literary accounts of the Soviet experience; and they attended political meetings. Then, however, the political energies of the Russian people seemed to dissipate. Instead of political engagement, Russians reverted to stoicism, apathy, and cynicism.

To begin to judge how accurate these perceptions are, we need to return to the dawn of Russia's democratization and inquire how new rules for the political game began to emerge in the absence of the single-party monopoly. One basic fact stands out: "democracy" was initially a mode of politics that was imposed by the Communist Party leadership, not one that the Russian people were out on the streets demanding. Consequently, the Party was able to have the first stab at defining what it entailed. *Demokratiya* was a term much used by Mikhail Gorbachev in 1987–88, but his sense of the word was by no means a liberal one. Rather, he harked back to a "Leninist" model of "socialist pluralism," or democracy *within* a single party. In his view, the Soviet governing elite had become ossified and incapable of finding creative modern solutions to the challenges – primarily economic – that the USSR was failing to meet. It was imperative to mobilize the energies of rank-and-file members of the Party. The first tentative dabble in democracy came with an announcement in March 1987 that elections in about 1 percent of constituencies would have multiple candidates.[1]

Another crucial means of reinvigorating the Party, and Soviet society in general, was to encourage more discussion of current social problems in the Soviet press. This kind of debate quickly went beyond queues and corruption to a sustained reevaluation of the Soviet past. Back in the 1950s and early 1960s, Nikita Khrushchev had launched a campaign of de-Stalinization that denounced the dictator's crimes against his own Party; over the following twenty years, however, this campaign had stalled and gone into reverse as the Soviet leadership preferred not to ask itself awkward questions. In 1987, these questions were raised once again by newspaper and journal editors mostly hand-picked by Gorbachev himself.

As everyone now knows, discussion quickly went beyond anything Gorbachev and his advisors had envisaged. People did not just suggest tinkering with the system, they proposed its radical overhaul or even its removal. Critical examination of the Soviet past extended ever further back in time until it reached the last sacred cow in the herd: Lenin himself.

Gorbachev was not at first dissuaded from his course by the signs of incipient ideological disintegration. He pressed on with his radical new step: the introduction of an elected Soviet assembly, the Congress of People's Deputies. This body was to have 2,250 members; 1,500 of them would be elected directly in constituencies where the number of candidates could in principle exceed one, while the remaining 750 would be drawn from lists submitted by various social organizations (in the first instance, the Communist Party itself, which was thereby guaranteed 100 places in the Congress for its Politburo and other leading lights). Elections to the Congress were held in March 1989 with exceptionally high levels of popular interest and participation: the turnout was close to 90 percent.

One of the key attributes of a democracy that the Soviet political system lacked as it emerged from seventy years of one-party dictatorship was a sense of what the general lines of political debate should be. In the early years of Gorbachev's political reforms (1987–89), one issue was constantly to the fore: should the liberalizing reforms be supported and deepened, or should they be rejected? Gorbachev's opponents argued vigorously that they were ill-conceived and bound to lead to a disastrous weakening of key Soviet institutions and of the Soviet Union itself (they were not wrong). Gorbachev's supporters argued that reform was the only way to shake out the stagnation from the Soviet system and to make it viable for the long term (they *were* wrong).

The spectrum of political opinion became even more stretched in the spring of 1990, when the Soviet Union saw its first fully con-tested elections – to parliaments at the level of individual Soviet republics. In the 1989 elections to the Soviet Congress, just under half of constituency seats had more than one candidate; in the 1990 Russian elections, the figure went as high as 97 percent.[2] Caught unawares by this snowballing of democracy, Gorbachev had been forced a few weeks before the elections to lift the monopoly of the Communist Party on political representation. In the new republican parliaments – including the Russian – he was anything but a hero: as the leading representative of central Soviet institutions, he was the main obstacle to democratically-based national sovereignty.

At this point the political landscape in Soviet Russia changed fundamentally. Now Gorbachev, the Communist Party reformer and democratizer, was opposed by "democrats" on the "left" as well as by "communists" on the "right." He was increasingly caught in the crossfire of the key political battle of the times (though, as the state he headed came under threat in 1990–91, he tended to side with the right in his desire to keep the USSR together).

The splitting of the Party into two warring factions gave rise to a great deal of vigorous if unstructured independent political activity. A democratic movement emerged out of the "informal organiza-tions" that sprang up and flourished from 1987 onward, when Soviet restrictions on freedom of assembly were substantially lifted. Many of these organizations – sports clubs, music societies, and so on – were apolitical, but a healthy minority were discussion clubs. The announcement of nationwide contested elections in 1989 gave the sprawling democratic movement the incentive to take sharper organ-izational form. Political clubs and citizen committees around the country campaigned vigorously on behalf of the democrats. Once the democrats had established a strong foothold in the Congress of People's Deputies, many of their deputies joined up to form a loose pro-reform coalition, the Interregional Deputies Group, which met for the first time in June 1989.

Until the beginning of 1990, the diversification of Soviet politics was still notionally occurring within a single party. The great majority of deputies elected to the Congress in March 1989 were members of the CPSU. A new, more openly pluralist kind of politics emerged rapidly at the start of 1990 in anticipation of the elections to the Russian Congress. In January 1990, various grassroots discussion groups and liberal factions from the CPSU formed a loose electoral bloc named "Democratic Russia." At this stage, democrats could afford to be vague about what divided them from one another (individuals differed on the question of whether they should abandon the CPSU entirely): they focused instead on their common opposition to hardline communism.

The democrats' opponents in the elections to the Russian Congress had also made some efforts to mobilize grassroots support for a more democratic kind of politics. In 1989, they had established a United Workers' Front to reclaim the proletarian base of support that they regarded as their birthright. When it came to the elections, however, they were hampered by their continued allegiance to a Soviet Communist Party that had lost much of its popular authority over the past couple of years and that – under Gorbachev's leadership – had been responsible for policies of which they themselves strongly disapproved. It was only after the elections, in June 1990, that conservative communist deputies formed their own, Russian, Communist Party, which was free of Gorbachev's liberal deviations. As a result, they became the largest faction in a Russian Congress that was polarized between communists and democrats. By early 1991, moreover, they were gaining further allies by moving closer to nationalists who also made the preservation of the USSR a key goal.

The democratic coalition held firm and eventually prevailed for a number of reasons. One was the politicization of the Russian population in its favor. The heavy-handed actions of the Soviet regime

– especially the brutal attempt to suppress separatism in the Baltic states in January 1991 – lost it yet more credibility. The collapse of living standards, attributable directly to the policies of the Soviet government, also played its part. Another important factor in the defeat of conservative communism was the charismatic revolutionary leadership of Boris Yeltsin, whose populist instincts equipped him well to ride the swelling wave of discontent with Soviet-style socialism. But the most important trigger for political resolution was the failure of the attempt by conservative communists to take over government by force in August 1991.

This decisive defeat of the communist establishment should have heralded the democrats' finest hour, but instead it marked the start of a period of political rudderlessness. The dominant issue of 1990–91 – communism or democracy – had been resolved, and the question now was simply: What next? The democratic movement up to this point had derived its unity and sense of purpose from its opposition to the USSR, but on closer inspection it comprised a group of politicians with wildly diverse ideas on such crucial matters as economic reform and nationality politics. Democratic Russia was a broad movement with an overarching cause rather than an organization with a coherent program. In the absence of any real political discipline, individuals had free rein to seek personal advantage: the bloc included numerous strong and ambitious personalities who wanted to capitalize on their own resources and reputations instead of diluting them in a common pool of party ideology. No one in the democrats' camp as yet had any practical evidence that negotiation, cooperation and compromise worked; their victory had been achieved as the outcome of contingency and confrontation.

Now that the period of crisis and combat was over, the democrats were faced by a number of more mundane but no less challenging tasks: how to work out what they stood for; where agendas and programs varied between different groups and individuals, how to determine whether those differences were important enough to be reflected in separate political organizations; and, in cases where they *were* considered significant, how to communicate them to an electorate. One of the less widely appreciated legacies of a one-party state is the absence of meaningful political labels for use in a democratic system. As we know from Western democracies, words like "republican," "liberal," and "conservative," although they certainly do not mean the same thing to all people at all times, form an effective shorthand that enables political parties to lobby for support or to create bogeymen. But this political vocabulary has been in continuous use in the West for at least two centuries, while post-communist Russia was to a large extent learning it from scratch.

There were a number of other reasons to believe that the learning process would be difficult. Mass democracy emerged in the West along with industrialization and working-class political representation. In other words, the language of politics had social class as its "carrier": at least some of the parties were able to draw on a powerful constituency in a broad, but reasonably well-defined, section of society. Russia, which had cut straight to state socialism without this slow maturation of class politics into electoral democracy, could not reckon on any easy correspondence between politics and class: for more than fifty years, ever since the proletariat had purportedly completed its victory over the bourgeoisie, classes were not officially recognized as having separate and antagonistic political interests. In post-Soviet politics it was not clear how political parties with no established track record – which was, of course, the case with all parties but one – would establish a social base. Initial signs were not good. The membership of the Democratic Party of Russia (one of the main parties to emerge from Democratic Russia) fell from 50,000 in early 1992 to around 15,000 at the end of the year.[3] In terms of grassroots activity, it appeared that the democratic movement had not moved on much from 1987 or 1988.

Perhaps the greatest single obstacle to the consolidation of democracy in Russia was that the victorious "democrats" never had the opportunity to face the hard discipline of political power. By 1992 the new Russian state was headed by a president who had always seemed sympathetic to the democratic movement but who never actually joined it or unambiguously endorsed it at key moments. His main political asset was not an ideology, a set of policies, or an independent political organization but his own status as a revolutionary hero, his personal charisma, and the abundant sources of power he had inherited from the old system. To the extent that he did make general pronouncements on political issues, he continued to invoke the now obsolete polarities – "communists versus democrats" – of the late Soviet period.

Under these circumstances the democrats, beset by personal rivalries at the best of times, began to fragment. Many of them formed part of a sprawling parliamentary coalition that increasingly railed against the president's high-handedness. Others directed their efforts toward building a pro-presidential party of government. This quest culminated in June 1993 in the creation of Russia's Choice, the first of several aspiring "parties of power" in Russian politics in the 1990s: a cluster of politicians with strong connections to government circles who aimed to provide the presidential executive with a bulwark in the legislative assembly. The problem, however, was that the creators of Russia's Choice did not carry with them all of the democrats or all the supporters of the president. They had to compete with two other prominent parties that had emerged from Democratic Russia (Yabloko, headed by the well-known economist Grigory Yavlinsky, and Nikolai Travkin's Democratic Party of Russia) as well as another candidate "party of power" (Sergei Shakhrai's Party of Russian Unity and Concord). The democrats were by now split on issues of substance: Yeltsin's increasingly authoritarian style of rule, the desirability of the Soviet collapse, the manner of the economic reforms. And, as they geared up for the first national elections in post-Soviet Russia, all the broadly "democratic" groupings had to face stiff competition from a resurgent Communist Party and a number of shifting unions between "centerists," nationalists, and Soviet statists.

In 1993 a bitter power struggle was fought between the president and the Supreme Soviet, but the new post-Soviet Russia did not have the chance to vote for either of them. Politicians occasionally presented the population with open-ended referendum questions, but remarkably little progress was made in packaging distinctive political programs to the electorate. As in 1991, political differences were resolved by force rather than through debate.

In December 1993, finally, came the foundational elections to the Russian legislature (renamed the Duma after Yeltsin's termination of the working life of the Supreme Soviet). According to the new rules, half of the 450 deputies were elected in single-member constituencies, while the others were chosen from party lists according to a system of proportional representation (with the proviso that a party had to reach a threshold of 5 percent of the vote to begin to receive seats). If parties in single-mandate constituencies had a party affiliation, they were not allowed to make this known on the ballot papers (a measure designed to blunt the power of the Communist Party, which had by far the greatest nationwide reach of all the contending parties). The registration period allowed little time for parties to gather the 100,000 signatures that were required of them, and the Central Electoral Commission enjoyed considerable discretion to disallow parties (especially, of course, those hostile to the president).

Despite all these prophylactic measures, the elections were a disaster for the would-be "party of power" and for the other successor parties to Democratic Russia. Russia's Choice, the group with all the enormous material benefits of official backing, obtained only 15.51 percent of PR votes and 13.70 percent of single-member seats (a total of seventy seats in the Duma). The Russian Communist Party, which enjoyed the significant advantage of "name recognition" amid all the ideological chaos, shrugged off presidential disapprobation to capture forty-eight Duma seats. But the best individual performance was certainly that of Vladimir Zhirinovsky, whose Liberal Democratic Party captured the party-list votes of more than 12 million Russians – and became the second largest party in the Duma with sixty-four seats – by pushing a radical nationalist message. Zhirinovsky had not been hampered either by government efforts to discredit him (which had only brought him more exposure) or by the tangential relationship of his party to liberal democracy.

Although the Duma was full of deputies propounding views at odds with presidential policies, the 1993 elections had not upset the balance of Russian politics: about half the deputies were broadly "democratic" (in that they basically accepted the necessity of political liberalization and market reform, even if not in precisely the ways these had been handled by Boris Yeltsin), while most of the rest were communist or nationalist opponents. The single most striking aspect of the 1993 elections was not Zhirinovsky's triumph but the fragmentation of Russian politics that made it possible. Thirteen parties ended up on the ballot papers, many of them distinguishable from each other only to experts (if at all). Eight of the thirteen ended up with a double-figure number of seats. The single greatest category in the Duma, however, was that of the "independents" who had run in the single-member seats: they accounted for 141 of 225 deputies elected in that half of the ballot.

Perhaps this complex fracture of the previous enforced unity was only to be expected at such an early stage of democratization, but the second post-Soviet Duma elections (held after a shortened first term, as scheduled, in December 1995) showed no signs of healing it: the number of parties went up to forty-two. Surveys suggested that 71 percent of voters who took part in the previous elections had switched parties since 1993 (in an established democracy the rate would usually be in the range 15–25 percent).[4] The changes in voter choice were primarily due not to the fickleness of the electorate but to the shifting range of parties on offer. The previous "party of power," Russia's Choice, had been replaced by Our Home Is Russia, a movement launched by Prime Minister Viktor Chernomyrdin in April 1995. Zhirinovsky's success had inspired others to try their hand at nationalism, which eroded his party's share of the Duma seats to fifty-one. These imitators most notably included the communists, who had moved decisively toward nationalism in 1994–95, continued to improve their grassroots organization, and became comfortably the largest single party in the Duma with 157 seats. However, their gains were largely at the expense of the equally unpalatable (to the reformers) Liberal Democratic and Agrarian Parties. They were not able to create a majority bloc in the Duma because of the impossibility of reaching a working arrangement with the Zhirinovsky camp.

What seems remarkable with hindsight is not the fact that the communists made a strong comeback in the mid-1990s but that this comeback did not sweep them back to power – and that they and other opponents of Yeltsin decided to play by rules that had been imposed on them by force by the president. The Duma and the president continued to have a strained relationship – moments of acute conflict came in February 1994, when the Duma infuriated Yeltsin by voting an amnesty for those prosecuted for participating in the

White House "events" of 1991 and 1993, and when the presidential administration, shocked by Zhirinovsky's success in 1993, attempted (unsuccessfully) to increase the number of single-mandate seats from 225 to 300 – but political life kept going nevertheless.

Opposition politicians were acquiescent partly because most of them were well schooled in political systems where elites, whatever their mutual antipathies, kept outsiders in their place and carved up power between themselves. They were pragmatic enough to realize that Duma seats gave them lobbying power and perks that were too valuable to be risked in another armed confrontation with the president. In addition, they were reckoning on the forthcoming presidential elections. Up to this point, the president had been able to shrug off the many electoral reverses of his sympathizers in the Duma: his executive powers were such that he could live with an uncooperative legislature. But the 1996 elections, the first of their kind in post-Soviet Russia, were something else entirely: to lose them would be to lose power comprehensively. Defeat for Yeltsin seemed overwhelmingly the most likely result at the start of the year, when his ratings were down to single figures. But he staged a remarkable comeback with the aid of mass media that were almost entirely on his side.

In the two subsequent presidential elections (in 2000 and 2004), Vladimir Putin enjoyed similar advantages and secured victory by wide margins. More strikingly, over the past two electoral cycles, the president managed to gain control over the Duma. In the 1999 elections, a vicious power struggle behind the scenes resulted in the sudden creation of a new party, Unity, that had its founding congress in October but in December received a staggering 15.5 million party-list votes and became the second largest grouping in the Duma. In 2003, this party, renamed as United Russia, strengthened its grip on the Duma to such an extent that some observers have spoken of one-party parliamentarism or of Bonapartist electoral dictatorship.

If Russian democracy seems flawed at the national level, it does so all the more at the local level, where Soviet elites were generally adept, after a few months submerged in the choppy waters of transition, at resurfacing in democratic politics. The first signs of democracy in the provinces came with relatively free elections to regional soviets (local agencies of state power) in the spring of 1990. In the autumn of 1993, Yeltsin decreed that these Soviet bodies be dissolved in all regions apart from the twenty-one republics and replaced by elected regional legislatures (the same process that was happening on a national level with the Duma elections). Although nine regional soviets were given special permission to serve out their full term (until 1995 or even 1996), legislative elections began to occur from December 1993 onward.

Elections for regional executives occurred early on in Moscow, St. Petersburg, and Tatarstan, but for the most part they took longer to catch on. Republics were allowed to choose their own arrangement: either to hold direct popular elections or to retain the quasi-parliamentary structures of the Soviet system (which meant that the chairperson of their Supreme Soviet would also be their chief executive). In the other regions, however, the centralized Soviet system of appointment was maintained at the start of the transition period: in 1991–92 their heads of administration were still chosen for them by Moscow. It was not until the spring of 1993 that the first executive elections occurred in places other than republics, at which point conflicts often arose between the elected governors and Yeltsin's appointees. The pace quickened in the second electoral cycle: sixteen elections for regional chief executives were held in the second half of 1995, and three times that number in 1996. By 2003, Dagestan was the only Russian region where direct elections for the chief executive had never occurred.[5]

By the end of the first post-Soviet decade, then, political life in even the most remote regions of the Russian Federation had the same democratic trappings as the center: elected executives and legislatures. Whether these amounted to democracy in any substantive sense is, however, open to much doubt. Parties at the regional level were even weaker than at the national. Their role in regional executive elections was tiny and, though greater in legislative elections, it still compared unfavorably with older democracies. According to the Central Electoral Commission, only 10 percent of deputies elected to regional legislatures between 1995 and 1997 were affiliated to the twelve largest parties in Russia. A further 10 percent operated under the aegis of regionally formed parties, which meant that 80 percent of such deputies ran independently of any kind of party or movement.[6]

The weakness of party development reflected the localized nature of politics: as regions sought to safeguard their own positions in a situation of economic and constitutional uncertainty, political programs and preoccupations inevitably remained local and autarkic. The other reason why parties developed slowly if at all was that incumbent regional elites did not need them. They already had political and economic resources that more or less guaranteed them success in any electoral contest. To affiliate themselves to a national or interregional party would mean voluntarily to compromise their own power. The Yeltsin administration had set the political tone by turning away from proceduralism and rule-making, and its lead was followed in the regions. Informal relationships were a more secure means of wielding power than more open forms of politicking. The complexity of political arrangements – and the contradictory and self-defeating character of formal political jurisdictions – was exacerbated by the opacity of Russian federalism and the often extended periods of "cohabitation" between locally elected governors and presidential appointees.

This is not to say that political outcomes were everywhere identical. Regional political regimes varied significantly in their constitutional arrangements: a few gave their presidents more or less dictatorial powers, others opted for a strong executive, while in still other cases effective power was shared between executive and legislature. But this did not mean that legislatures were necessarily responsive to public opinion: the work of these regional assemblies was structured by unaccountable committees, not by openly constituted parties. Where parties did come into being, they tended to reflect divisions within the incumbent political elite rather than any broader social movement. Politics was less about attitudes to democracy than about the struggle for resources.[7]

A study of politics in Russia's regions, then, shows that democratization was by no means the only, or even the most "rational," outcome of the removal of one-party control. In these conditions it made far more sense for elites to share out the power they already had instead of gambling on democratic parties that would be costly to set up and maintain and be of dubious political efficacy. In this context, regular elections were rarely a hindrance to the operation of informal institutions. The word "democrat" in Russian was a linguistic leftover from the struggle against Soviet centralism in 1990–91. In post-Soviet conditions it continued to be used intensively, though its relationship to democracy was often spurious. To be a "democrat" usually meant an acceptance of economic reform and an assumption that urban elites – managerial, bureaucratic, or technocratic depending on the location – knew better than their electorates.

Can anything be said against this bleak view of the democratic deficit of post-Soviet Russia? Are Russians anything more than the unsuspecting dupes, or the disempowered victims, of a new form of authoritarianism? Did democracy matter to Russians?

One way of approaching these questions is to ask whether Russians felt the need to vote. Turnout for national elections was by no means high by European standards but nor was it completely out of line with patterns in modern democracies. The lowest figure in the 1990s was for the Duma election and constitutional plebiscite of December 1993: only 54.37 percent of eligible voters were reported to have cast their ballots at a time when the legitimacy of Russian political institutions was at its weakest. In 1995 the figure rose to 64.37 percent, and it was higher still for both rounds of the presidential elections in 1996 (just under 70 percent).

What of the notion that biased media prevented Russians from becoming active citizens? It is certainly true that electoral politics was conducted primarily through the mass media. Russia had acquired mass democracy at a much later stage than Western countries and lacked traditions of door-to-door canvassing and grassroots campaigning. By the mid-1990s, television was overwhelmingly the most important medium. In an average week of campaigning before the 1995 and 1996 elections, 85 percent of the electorate followed events on television, while only 50 percent or so got their information from newspapers. But access to airtime was highly inequitable. In the run-up to the 1995 Duma elections, the government-sponsored party, Our Home Is Russia, was able to buy almost seventy-five times more of it than the Communists. [8] Critical views of the incumbent regime – even after Putin became president – were abundantly available on the internet, but even in 2000 only a few million Russians were active users. Even if the more wired-up citizens did read and disseminate oppositional opinion, it was unlikely to have any great impact: what the web gained in range of opinion, it lost in coherence and direct political impact.

Yet it would be incorrect (not to mention patronizing) to assume that Russians were straightforwardly deceived by the Yeltsinite propaganda served up on TV. Of course, Russians were affected by what they saw on their screens, but we should not exaggerate the gullibility of a population that was used to being lied to. After all, Our Home Is Russia did not receive a number of votes commensurate with the media bias in its favour: its share of the party-list vote was under half of the communists'.

It might be objected that a similarly extreme imbalance in media coverage swung the crucial 1996 presidential elections in Yeltsin's favor. Even in this case, however, Russian voters were not ignorant or ingenuous: as the opinion polls consistently showed, they were by no means blind to the failings of their leader. Although Yeltsin made long overdue nods in the direction of public opinion – notably by showing signs of bringing the first Chechen war to a negotiated end – these do not appear to have been the crucial swing factor. Nor did Russians vote their president back in from a sense of indifference or resignation. It seems rather that there were certain aspects of the post-communist transformation they were not about to jettison: a critical mass of voters broadly accepted the inevitability of the market reforms that the main alternative to Yeltsin – the communist Zyuganov – had promised to reverse. It is hard otherwise to explain why Russia bucked the trend of post-communist states and did *not* vote back into power a revamped socialist party after suffering a few years of market reforms. This fact is all the more remarkable given that the decline in living standards was much more drastic in the former Soviet Union than in other parts of Eastern Europe. In one public opinion survey, only about 15 percent of respondents in 1996 felt themselves to be "winners" of transition while almost half considered that they had lost out. Public opinion research suggested that to pit unrepentant communists against democratic reformers was seriously to underestimate the true complexity of attitudes. In reality, Russians were quite capable of being egalitarian and statist while at the same time approving, or at least accepting, the free market and political pluralism. They believed in social "floors" but were disinclined to impose too low a "ceiling": attitudes to the accumulation of wealth had turned a corner since the late Soviet era.[9]

Yeltsin's victory in 1996 may thus be seen less as a reflection of positive support for him, or even of media manipulation, than as evidence of how genuinely unpalatable the alternative was to a small but sufficient majority of voters. Unlike voters in other parts of Eastern Europe, Russians did not have the alternative of a Communist Party that had reshaped itself in the mold of Western-style social democracy. They were faced with an unappealing choice between bad and worse.

It is often said that Russians' lack of civic virtues such as trust and cooperation makes them especially vulnerable to presidential scaremongering against the communists and incapable of mounting a serious grassroots challenge to political elites. However, the contrast between the Russians and their purportedly trusting and civically minded Western counterparts is overdrawn. In a 1998 survey, for example, Russian respondents came across as full of suspicion: nearly 60 percent of them said that "one cannot be too cautious," while only 30 percent said that their fellow citizens could be trusted. Yet, when compared with other European countries, Russia's trust rating placed it somewhere in the middle of the range: Spain, France and Portugal were lower, as (by a greater margin) were most countries in Central and Eastern Europe.[10]

But if we look more specifically at attitudes to the institutions of public life, trust in Russia is disastrously (if also justifiably) low. Post-Soviet politicians never enjoyed high repute, but from the mid-1990s onward popular cynicism extended from them to the media that reported their words and doings. The problem was less that people were deceived by what they saw on television than that they were distrustful of everything that journalists said. All journalists were widely perceived to be in the pay of one special interest or another. This was partly the consequence of emerging from a closed society where all information was centrally coordinated: far from brainwashing people into taking the state at its word, it made them inclined to disbelieve just about everything they heard. Regrettably, journalists themselves served up ample material for even the least committed post-communist conspiracy theorists. Just as Boris Yeltsin made a Faustian pact with the oligarchs in 1996 to secure reelection, so the "free" Russian media compromised their journalistic integrity by foisting the president on the population and blackening his opponents.

Perhaps the least discouraging thing that could be said about democracy in Yeltsin's Russia was that it was still very early in its life, and that, given its troubled infancy, the current situation could have been worse. Mikhail Gorbachev and Boris Yeltsin were sworn political enemies, but as political leaders they had at least one thing in common: they both missed opportunities to consolidate democracy at moments that were favorable to them (Gorbachev by failing to put himself up for popular election as president in 1990, Yeltsin by not calling new elections for the Supreme Soviet after August 1991). What this meant, in both cases, was that the next phase of political transformation was achieved by violent, non-democratic means. In the language of comparative transitology, Russia's was emphatically not a "pacted" transition to democracy. Conflicting political elites did not manage to negotiate new rules of the political game; rather, these rules remained unclear until they were imposed unilaterally (and often by force).

This was not just a matter of the pig-headedness of Yeltsin and his opponents. It was also to do with the fact that Russian political groups had much more fundamental areas of disagreement than their counterparts in Eastern Europe. For example, they could not even agree in 1992–93 over what country they were supposed to be governing. Nor could they repudiate communism in the same way as the Czechs or the Poles. At a time when other post-communist societies were debating exactly what transition path to take, Russia was still preoccupied with the question of whether transition from communism was desirable at all. Nor were Russians able to use history to forge a sense of common purpose: the communist era – especially the Brezhnev years, but in some ways even Stalinism – could not be seen in the same somber light in which they appeared to many Eastern Europeans who had just thrown off Soviet suzerainty.

At the end of 1993 the ground rules of the political system were more or less established, and most politicians started to abide by them. But there remained a troubling mismatch between political power and democratic representation. The main power-holders fought shy of party politics. Yeltsin never joined a party, and the various "parties of power" (the groupings that aligned themselves with the Kremlin and ran in the Duma elections) performed consistently badly. The pattern was set as early as 1990, when the first multiparty elections occurred just weeks after the Communist Party gave up its monopoly on party politics. The political struggle was already in full swing, and the building of well-defined parties was always a secondary preoccupation.

The design of the new political system also did little to encourage party formation. Staggered presidential and parliamentary elections contributed to a political climate where the incumbent president never needed to tie his fortunes to a party. The majority runoff system (whereby the top two candidates in the first round ran against each other in the second) meant that small parties were not discouraged from running even if they had no chance of success, because they could trade their support for ministerial posts and other perks. Even the PR system for Duma elections, which might be expected to strengthen parties, did not have this effect: given the strong apartisan president, PR encouraged ambitious politicians to use political parties as a stepping stone to something greater. The parliamentary elections of the mid-1990s have been described as the Russian equivalent of US presidential primaries: as an opportunity for politicians to tout their wares as potential future presidents.[11]

The focus of Russian politicians on short-term tactical gain rather than long-term strategy was reflected in their taste for extreme organizational flexibility. Parties were by no means the only genre of political organization: the others included movements, association, unions, leagues, congresses, foundations, and fronts. Before the 1993 elections, thirty-five associations of various kinds presented lists of candidates and signature sheets to the electoral commission, but only thirteen were allowed to stand for election (and only five of these carried the nomenclature of "party"). In 1995, a staggering 111 organizations attempted to get on to the ballot, only thirty-eight of them parties.[12] By the early twenty-first century, in the era of Putin and Unity, the "electoral bloc" was a particularly successful instrument of electoral politics: it brought together political groupings at short notice to maximum electoral effect without necessarily committing its members to long-term collaboration or implying a common ideology. Individual parties could not begin to compete for sheer electoral outreach. In the 1999 Duma elections, only three parties had the resources to put up candidates in as many as 100 of the 250 single-member districts.[13]

The lack of transparency in Russian electoral politics was exacerbated by the drafting and enforcement of electoral legislation, which gave the state ample discretion to disqualify political parties for infringing draconian rules on electoral registration. In 1999, a new federal law on the Duma elections to be held in December was signed only in mid-June, but it required parties wishing to participate in the PR ballot to hand in – by October 24 – lists with 200,000 signatures by eligible voters (with the further restriction that no more than 7 percent of these voters could be resident in a any single region). An alternative was to raise a cash deposit of a little more than $80,000, but the Central Electoral Commission could still find capricious grounds to exclude individual candidates from the party lists. At the same time, effective control over campaign spending was loose in the extreme: for the 1999 elections the sums disbursed officially amounted to $15 million, which was certainly a ludicrous underestimate.[14]

Both at the national and the regional level, post-Soviet Russian politics illustrates the historical lesson that politicians choose multi-party democracy not out of the goodness of their hearts but because it is in their interests to do so. In Russia in the 1990s, it was in too many people's interests for democracy to remain weak.

That said, a case can be made that significant changes in Russian politics have occurred since Putin came to power in 1999. At the time, the unexpectedly strong showing of Unity seemed to be yet another unwelcome indication of the ease with which the executive could manipulate the democratic process – and of the extent to which purportedly "democratic" politics reflected more power struggles in the elite than any weight of popular opinion. Unity was yet another "party of power" and had been specially engineered to weaken the vote of a party led by former Kremlin insiders who happened to have lost Yeltsin's favor. Party fragmentation continued: of the twenty-six parties slated for the 1999 elections, nineteen were new arrivals since 1995, and the turnover of candidates for the presidential elections of the following year was similarly high.

Yet, although Unity was not the first party to receive presidential endorsement and privileged access to the media, it was the first of its kind to make real headway in Duma elections. Clearly it had got right things that Russia's Choice and Our Home Is Russia had got wrong. It offered a vigorous, youthful leadership in place of presidential cronies like Viktor Chernomyrdin. It made a successful pitch for new, apolitical voters by carefully avoiding ideology and professing a vague "centerism." Instead of grand statements of political intent, it sent out signals of pragmatism and professionalism: its stated aim was to put an end to a decade of bickering between president and parliament and achieve a stable and productive working relationship between the two. The other key ingredient was patriotism boosted by the start of the second Chechen war. All these carefully chosen messages were adroitly directed at the electorate by a media campaign that chose as the movement's mascot a bear – a convenient symbol of the "Russian" virtues of strength and common sense that Unity wanted to project.

With six years of hindsight, the 1999 Duma elections seem to have marked some sort of shift in Russian political culture. They were the first significantly de-ideologized elections of the post-communist era. The questions of whether the territorial boundaries of the Russian Federation should be redrawn or extended and whether state socialism should be reimposed, were no longer relevant. In the 2003 elections these trends went much further. Unity merged with politicians from a rival party of power, renamed itself United Russia, and gained a stranglehold over the Duma. The more ideologically minded *perestroika* generation of Russian politicians seemed to be fading from the scene: they were well represented among the 54 percent of deputies who failed to retain their seats. The communists made another respectable showing, but their vote was now starting to tail off as their core electorate aged, and they no longer constituted a real political threat to the incumbent regime. The Liberal Democrats, whose fortunes had declined in the second half of the 1990s as Zhirinovsky's charisma seemed to pall, made something of a comeback. The liberals were as divided as ever, and their taste for elaborate programs was out of tune with the times: as a result, they all but dropped off the political map (though there was some hope they might reappear as a remote island republic if they ever consolidated their personnel). The electorate appeared more apathetic and disenchanted than ever. Turnout returned to the miserable level of December 1993, and almost 5 percent of those completed ballot papers contained votes "against all candidates."[15]

Unity's politics of consolidation succeeded not only because it was skillfully conducted but because the times were right for it. By 1999 a consensus had been established in Russian society about the inevitability of the status quo and the preferability of gradual over radical change – a consensus that bridged all the great divides of Russian society (age, sex, education, wealth).[16] This marked a change from the mid-1990s, when survey results revealed clear generational cleavage across all of post-communist Eastern Europe on the question of the desirability of market reform.[17] By the end of the decade, certain matters of principle – notably the relative merits of communism and capitalism – were no longer burning issues.

But this was an electorate still afraid that radical change might be foisted upon it. Fear levels before the 2000 presidential elections were lower than in 1996 but still astounding by the standards of more stable political systems: 24 percent of survey respondents said they feared civil war as a result of the elections (as compared with 45 percent four years earlier), and 38 percent were bracing themselves for a drastic economic downturn. But Russians were not in favor of strong-arm methods to reduce uncertainty. Democracy was still something they believed in. Nearly nine out of ten Russians at around the same time believed voting to be a civic duty. Shortly after the 2000 presidential elections, four out of five respondents in one survey declared that democracy in Russia was desirable. Nor were they under many illusions about the present state of affairs:

only one in five thought Russia could be considered a democratic country at the present moment. [18]

The crucial question, however, is what exactly "democracy" was held to mean. During the 1990s, the word had given itself a thoroughly bad name as the Yeltsin regime acquiesced in cronyism and "comprador capitalism." By 2000, many Russians had come to feel that democracy should – and, more importantly, could – have more institutional steel to it. In practice, while trust in political institutions remained weak, this meant having faith in the powers of one man to put them in order. In a 2003 survey, almost 60 percent of respondents expressed complete trust in the president, but only 5 percent in political parties and 9 percent in the State Duma.[19]

The Putin era thus saw a partial return to Soviet-style paternalist thinking, though it is important to recognize that the Russian population was not wrong to distrust political institutions. But the beneficiary of this paternalist turn – Vladimir Putin – was a new kind of leader for Russia, much as he drew on know-how and political capital he had accumulated under the *ancien régime*. By this time, Putin could plausibly be described by two British scholars as a "Russian Tony Blair" – if it is possible to imagine a Tony Blair who learned his law in the KGB rather than in bar school.[20] "Centerism" (a distant cousin of the "third way") was the closest he came to an ideology. He also showed signs of adopting important mannerisms of "modern" political leadership. In August 2000, when the submarine *Kursk* went down and stayed down at the cost of more than 100 lives, Putin made no televisual gestures of human concern; four years later, after the catastrophe of the hostage crisis in Beslan, he reacted much more promptly, delivering an address to the nation that was heavy with political significance. For the most part, he appeared to be steering a successful middle course between those Russian leaders who had been too uncommunicative (Brezhnev and Yeltsin) and those who had talked too much to maintain the respect of the population (Khrushchev and Gorbachev).

Another truly novel aspect of the Putin era was the fact that a Russian president began to see that a political system with a small number of well-established parties (or pseudo-parties) could work in his favor. At times Putin even took steps to prevent Russian politics looking too outrageously one-sided. He bolstered the liberal Yabloko party – by offering valuable airtime to its leader – and appears to have been genuinely surprised when it failed to clear the 5 per-cent threshold in 2003. He also took strong measures to increase party consolidation in the politically fragmented Russian provinces. After publicly bemoaning the weakness of the Russian party system, Putin pushed through a new Law on Political Parties in June 2001. According to its stipulations, a party had to demonstrate much greater regional penetration than was currently the norm: it was to have local organizations in more than half of Russia's regions along with a total membership of at least 10,000 (with the further requirement that these members should not be spread too thinly over the regions). In 2002, a further law imposed restrictions on the electoral systems the regions could adopt and on their electoral procedures, again with the aim of opening up the closed political arena of the provinces to the federal government.[21]

Putin's legislative changes have often been radical on paper, but it is questionable whether they have brought profound changes. For all his rhetorical insistence on the importance of law, Putin has the same taste for top-down ad hoc measures as so many Russian rulers before him. In September 2004, for example, he demolished one potential pillar of regional democracy by decreeing that he would nominate regional leaders instead of allowing them to be elected locally. His attempts to bolster political parties in the Russian provinces reflected above all his ambition to use them as instruments of control, not any commitment to political pluralism. By bringing regional elites into stable national parties, he could reduce the potential for unruliness of individual subjects of the federation. Yet, like all his predecessors, he found that strong central government had a limited reach and was obliged to enter deals with sometimes unsavory provincial bosses. Putin's first reappointee after the new legislation of September 2004 was the shady Sergei Darkin, a man with known links to organized crime, in the notoriously corrupt Far Eastern province. At the same time as Putin was attempting to get tough with provincial governors, moreover, United Russia was employing a less confrontational means of drawing comfortably ensconced regional elites into national politi-cal life: by offering them a piece of the action in Moscow.

Putin's "managed democracy," then, can be seen as the latest – and perhaps culminating – stage in Russia's transition from communism to Something Else. It is clear that the process of political change in Russia has been elite-driven to an extent exceptional in post-communist Eastern Europe. The main political institutions of post-Soviet Russia – Duma, presidential administration, elections, parties – have not come into being as a result of pressure from below. Nor have they had much to do with ideological cleavages. Political change has come about as elites have tried to convert their resources – many of them inherited from the old system – into the new currency of "democratic" institutions. At times, both at the national level and in the regions, this process has led to genuine conflict and uncertainty – notably in Yeltsin's numerous clashes with the Duma. But this conflict at no stage represented a "normal" pluralistic competition for power. It involved a trial of strength between different contenders for power. Sometimes one set of contenders were in a position to impose their will on all the others; on many occasions they were not, and the consequence was a period of pragmatic jostling or of tentative alliance building. In the Putin era, rival political groups are more likely to know their place. Executive and legislative are in synch, and the political elite appears to have reached a stable working arrangement. It remains highly unresponsive to signals "from below" such as campaigns by NGOs and pressure groups, which it tends to dismiss as a fifth column for Western meddlers. Successful lobbying seems to depend almost entirely on getting the ear of the right person in the presidential administration.

This is a "supply-side" problem more than a "demand-side" problem. The survey evidence suggests that many Russians understand what a fairer democracy would feel like and know rather better than most Westerners how far their own country falls short of this ideal. Russia's current predicament cannot be written off as the result of a genetic predisposition to authoritarianism. It results directly from the distribution of power and resources at the critical moment when the new Russia came into being and began its political life.

When we talk about "transition," then, we can now be confident that Russia has moved away from communism, but it is equally clear that Russia has not arrived at a destination named "democracy" (as this concept was conceived by upbeat transitologists in the first half of the 1990s). Russia bears eloquent witness to the fact that democracy does not come into being automatically just because a previous system of authoritarian rule collapses. This outcome also has to be in the interest of ruling elites. Nor do free and open elections necessarily undermine the interests of a ruling class with paternalist and authoritarian predilections. After all, they worked in Bismarck's favor in the 1870s.

The point would seem to have even greater force in the post-modern era of mass media, when incumbent politicians can add to their already formidable arsenal the black arts of the spin doctor. Contemporary Russia is a realization of every thinking citizen's worst feelings about the fakeness of modern mass-media democracy. The sense that political contestation – however much orange juice hits the walls of TV studios in tempestuous discussion programs – is largely for public display and is designed to conceal the more serious struggle for collective resources that is taking place behind the scenes. Russia can plausibly be seen as a "virtual," not a real democracy.[22]

Yet a number of counterarguments can be made against this gloomy assessment. One is that the social and economic base for effective democracy is yet to arrive in Russia. The social foundation of democracy everywhere has been an urban, educated, reasonably affluent middle class. The Russian population has been too buffeted by economic uncertainty for such a group to consolidate itself, but when it does, political life will become more vibrant and more liberal. For the time being, Russians' illiberal voting choices derive from a sense of insecurity rather more deeply rooted in reality than the fears – immigration, family breakdown, crime, terrorism – that are commonly expressed by illiberal citizens in the West.

Another more sanguine intellectual move is to invoke the law of unintended consequences. To be sure, Putin is currently seeking to strengthen political parties and play by more of the rules for more of the time because such steps in the direction of "normal" democracy are in his own political interests. But the forms of democracy may well take on more meaning in the future, when the President's ability to control the situation declines. If serious divisions within the elite reemerge, political parties may once again play the democratic game – but with more serious intent. Putin or his successor could face opposition in the Duma that is more effectively channeled than it was in the 1990s (when opposition votes and politicians were fragmented into dozens of parties and self-motivated interest groups).

For the medium term, however, it seems that Russia is likely to remain stuck with some form of "managed democracy": the current system is just too convenient for too many interest groups for it to receive a radical challenge. If significant change occurs, moreover, it is far from guaranteed to take a more liberal direction. It is not impossible that, instead of Putin "managing" democracy, "democracy" might start to manage Putin. By this I mean not that the president and his advisors will be forced to listen to voices from a burgeoning civil society but rather that they will come to depend increasingly on the statist nationalists who have made enormous strides in electoral politics over the last few years (though no longer in the obsolete guise of the Communist Party but in that of various "patriotic" groupings who travel much lighter in ideological terms). The vague "patriotism" of United Russia and other influential political groupings is a cover for all manner of special interests that are based largely in the army, the security apparatus and the military–industrial sector: over the long term, it is unlikely that one man, or even one presidential administration, will be able to keep these interests at arm's length. Even Putin's most committed critics would probably agree that a Russian Tony Blair, however statist and authoritarian in his instincts and his political practice, is still by no means the worst conceivable outcome for Russia's transition to illiberal democracy.

4 | Birth of a nation?

Although the Soviet state declined sharply at the start of the 1990s, Western apprehensions did not follow its steep downward trajectory. Communism had fallen as a political system and a dominant ideology, but that did not mean it could not be replaced by something just as malevolent toward prosperous liberal democracy. According to one prominent school of geopolitical thought, the "Russian bear" was bound to emerge from its debilitated hibernation before long; unless clear signals were given – notably through NATO enlargement – Russia would start once again to assert itself at the expense of Eastern European neighbors that it continued, at bottom, to regard as vassals. The notion of a revived Russian menace was lent further support by evidence of right-wing extremism in what appeared to be a dangerously destabilized political system. Western observers paid close attention to public demonstrations by assorted groups of fascists, antisemites, and Russian chauvinists. They shuddered at the electoral success of the ranting Russian imperialist, Vladimir Zhirinovsky. Not unreasonably, they supposed that radical, xenophobic nationalism was likely to hold great appeal in a society enduring immense hardship and humiliation.

Yet, for all their plausibility, these fears were not entirely borne out by the history of the first post-Soviet decade. To understand why the "Weimar Russia" scenario did not come about, to account for the failure of nationalism to radicalize post-Soviet Russia, we need first to take a few steps back in time and inquire what kind of Russian "nation" might have been expected to emerge from a state (the USSR) to which it bore a somewhat oblique relation.

The Soviet Union was a state, but not as we know it. To be sure, it met the main criteria for statehood: it had stable frontiers, an army, a bureaucracy, a set of centralized political institutions, and a monopoly on legitimate violence that it was not slow to use. Yet it also steadfastly resisted, or sidestepped, the greatest single determining factor in twentieth-century statehood: decolonization. The major European empires were either finished or brought to their knees by World War I; World War II applied the *coup de grâce* where it was needed. These empires were replaced by dozens of new states that could claim national self-determination as their principal source of legitimacy.

In this light, the Soviet Union appears a strange anachronism. Although the Russian Empire collapsed thunderously in 1917, over the next two decades most of its territory was reincorporated into a new state where many of its peoples suffered worse oppression than they had ever experienced under the tsars.

So was the Soviet Union no more than a modernized and brutalized version of the Russian Empire? Not entirely. It declared itself to be emphatically an internationalist and multinational state rather than an empire, and, although this self-description was often belied by Soviet policy on nationalities, it was slightly more than a communist con-trick or a piece of self-delusion.

The Bolsheviks took very seriously the problems of ruling an enormously diverse multiethnic population. They were aiming for a socialist state that would not be beset by any of the conflict – class or ethnic – that appeared to be endemic in modernizing societies elsewhere in Europe. One solution to the nationality problem was coercion: to tell people that they had no business being Ukrainians or Tatars or Bashkirs and that they should become Soviet citizens in short order. The Soviet regime was not shy to take the heavy-handed approach – usually in cases where ethnic groups occupied a particularly sensitive geopolitical position, such as the Ukrainians did in the early 1930s.

But there was more to Soviet nationalities policy than violence. The Bolsheviks operated with a theory of historical progress whereby the tensions and contradictions of bourgeois society would in due course put capitalism out of business. Nationalism was a pervasive by-product of bourgeois state-building. National identity was the only effective way for unjust, exploitative bourgeois societies to hold themselves together in the face of crushing oppression and inequality. Its strength had been shown at the outset of World War I, but this destructive conflict had also demonstrated to Marxists that nationalism was not, could not be, the end-point of history.

More recent theorists of nationalism would agree with the Bolsheviks that state-building greatly increases the scope and power of national identity. Railways, universal conscription armies, mass education, free trade, and mass media all have the effect of breaking down traditional communities and pushing people to take on broader allegiances. The territory of the former Russian Empire, however, contained a large number of regions that had experienced few if any of these modernizing developments. After much debate in the Civil War period, the Bolsheviks concluded that the backward areas of the Soviet Union should be put on a fast track to nationality, and that a policy of "indigenization" was the best way to accelerate their entry into the internationalist Soviet state. What this meant, among other things, was that territorial units at all levels of the Soviet administrative pyramid might proclaim a distinct national identity. If one village was officially Mordvinian, the next might be Chuvash, and the one after might be Russian.

Yet, for all that the early Soviet state has been identified by one perceptive historian as the "affirmative action empire," it was not pursuing indigenization out of any concern for fairness.[1] Its vision of the multiple new national groups was profoundly coercive. Once put on the fast track of historical progress, these emerging nationalities were expected to meet an exacting timetable: in due course they would merge with each other into ever-larger ethnic units, and after that they would come to recognize themselves as Soviet and socialist. Moreover, Soviet federalism was much more impressive on paper than in political reality. The party-state would happily trample on any ethnic group that stepped out of line or seemed to pose a threat. It also promoted national chauvinism when that seemed to meet its goals of social consolidation or political mobilization. For this reason, the Russians were firmly established by the mid-1930s as most favored nationality.

Nevertheless, this was not an empire in the sense that had been known hitherto. Although the regime regularly reduced the civil rights of various categories of the population, it did so more often on social and political criteria other than ethnicity. The Soviet Union did not have any nationality as its titular head. Although the Russians dominated both numerically and culturally, they did not have the political trappings of nationhood. Conversely, dozens of smaller ethnic groups that before 1917 had little if any administrative salience were now granted recognition as autonomous republics or regions.

When the Soviet Union started to come apart in the late 1980s, it had to confront in a hurry all the long-deferred problems of decolonization. How was the process to be managed so that it did not lead to bloody strife in dozens of regions where different ethnic groups might have competing claims? Who was to decide what kind of "nation" could go ahead and constitute its own state? The USSR had been so thorough in turning "nationality" into a key administrative category of its federal system that there were now well over 100 ethnic groups waiting in the wings – who was to say they would not now leap out on stage and demand full political independence? What was the best way to avert the prospect of violent disintegration? To maintain the USSR at all costs? To let all federal units go their separate ways? To adopt some more differentiated set of policies?

In the event, the cases of the "smaller" national republics at the union level turned out to be relatively straightforward, if far from painless. These nations – their peoples or their political leaders – did at least know what they wanted. The Baltic states, which had never begun to accept the legitimacy of Soviet-Russian hegemony, sought and achieved full independence after surviving attempts from within the Soviet establishment to keep them in the USSR by force. The Central Asian republics of the USSR took up the opportunity of independence but at the same time sought to retain the economic and political benefits of a close working relationship with the "center." Ukraine overwhelmingly chose independence at the end of 1991, though its relationship with Moscow was shifting and ambivalent.

The really difficult question, rather, was what would become of the "center" of the USSR when the peripheries sought new company. For Estonians and Ukrainians and Kazakhs, the modernizing Soviet state had acted as an incubator of national consciousness (even, or especially, when it had attempted to repress that consciousness). It had insisted that nationality was a salient feature of a Soviet citizen, it had promoted members of hitherto underrepresented national groups to positions of administrative responsibility, and it had created a full range of national political institutions in the various republics. These institutions were politically toothless while the Soviet system was still strong, but they were in a position to bite the system back if it ever weakened to a critical extent.

The one republic in the USSR that lacked a range of key institutions was Russia (the RSFSR). It had no KGB of its own, no Academy of Sciences and, most crucially, no Communist Party. It was itself a federation consisting of eighty-eight administrative units, more than thirty of which bore the name of a non-Russian ethnic group. Russian nationhood had been kept in the shadows by decades of Soviet nationality policy. When the Soviet federal state unraveled, the seceding nations had no trouble defining themselves (and, in many cases, wasted no time in passing discriminatory legislation against other national groups – notably Russians – within their borders). Russia, however, could only really be defined as a residue: as the Soviet Union shorn of its substantial peripheries. Of course, ethnic and cultural incoherence were not new problems for Russian nationhood: they had been a defining feature of it since the earliest times. But for the past few centuries they had generally been overcome or alleviated by maintaining a powerful state. In the early 1990s, however, the Russian state seemed anything but powerful. What, then, was to become of the nation? The question perennially debated, and often belabored, by Russian intellectuals was once again impossible to ignore: what *was* Russia?

All this will perhaps sound suspiciously like an apologia for Russian chauvinism. Can the Russians in the Soviet Union be considered victims in any meaningful sense, given that there appear to be so many stronger candidates for this designation? It is certainly true that Russians enjoyed the status of first among equals, and that the even-handed internationalism of Soviet ideology was evident more in the breach than in the observance. At times of stress and insecurity – notably the 1930s and World War II – Soviet leaders fell back on the trusty rhetorical resource of bombastic Russian-infused Great Power nationalism. But they took up Russian nationalism primarily because it was useful to them in creating a broader Soviet patriotism, not because it was a core value of the Soviet state.

In the 1960s and 1970s, the regime was once again receptive to Russian nationalism. By now the challenge was not to mobilize the population for a life-and-death struggle but to breathe life into the drooping ideology of Marxism-Leninism. At all levels of government in the RSFSR a new generation of administrators was coming to the fore: in the minds of these men, the great *Russian* victory of 1945 was a more meaningful event than the socialist triumph of 1917. They also resented what they might in another culture have identified as the excessive "political correctness" of Soviet nationalities policy, and started to lobby for more central resources to be channeled toward Russia.

These nationalist proclivities in the *apparat* were joined by a different kind of Russophilia in the intellectual elite. In the mid-1950s, the Party started to send out more liberal signals to writers; at the same time, the de-Stalinization campaign opened up an ideological void. Writers and literary critics responded to this situation by choosing themes and styles that would previously have seemed offbeat or politically dubious. In particular, by focusing on the predicament of the post-Stalin Russian village, they made a case for a rural Russianness that had been pushed to the brink of destruction by the depredations of the Stalin era.

For some writers of a nationalist persuasion, this rediscovery of rural roots was merely the first step toward a more radical assertion of Russian distinctiveness. They argued that military might and a strong centralized state were essential unchanging features of Russianness, and thus saw a direct continuity from medieval Rus through Muscovy and the Russian Empire all the way to the USSR. At the end of the 1960s, the regime made common cause with these "statist" Russian nationalists in a campaign against nationalists of a more liberal bent. By the end of the Brezhnev era, moreover, statist nationalism had gained a high degree of official toleration and even approval. The Soviet regime was happy to overlook its notional abhorrence of nationalism in the interests of political cohesion and mobilization. After all, a significant number of influential intellectuals were offering themselves as willing accomplices just as the socialist project was flagging. This was too good an opportunity for the regime to pass over.

The problem, however, was that overt Russian nationalism remained taboo within the political elite – and that, as time went on, the nationalist tail appeared increasingly to be wagging the socialist dog. Approved nationalist intellectuals did not always, or only, take a "Red" statist line. They might also, by idealizing the pre-Soviet past and expressing ambivalence toward the Soviet experience, betray "White" proclivities. Leonid Brezhnev and his ideology chief Mikhail Suslov had tended to be protective of the nationalists, but they both departed the scene in the early 1980s. For the next few years, the fortunes of the nationalists would fluctuate according to the balance of power and opinion in the party leadership. The arrival of Mikhail Gorbachev brought some cause for optimism. The youthful new General Secretary had a rural background and started his period as leader by taking up causes dear to the nationalists: agriculture, the environment, alcoholism. But he soon parted company with them as his *perestroika* took a more overtly liberalizing and democratizing direction.

When this occurred, the nationalist intellectuals found themselves in the vanguard of the first ever public and legal opposition movement in Soviet history. They argued with ever-ascending shrillness that Gorbachev's reforms constituted an abject capitulation to despised Western (which often, in their parlance, meant Jewish) concepts such as free-market liberalism and democracy. As signs of unrest in the Caucasus and the Baltic states multiplied, they directed their rhetorical energies toward maintaining the USSR, a state that for them was incontrovertibly the inheritor of Russia's historical destiny.

Here we come directly up against a major difference between Russia and all other cases of nation-building in post-communist Eastern Europe. The main card-carrying nationalists in the USSR were people who had prospered and come to prominence in a system designed to transcend the nation-state; and, at the very moment that system was showing weakness, they formed an opposition not to hasten its demise and bring forward the creation of a nationally defined state but rather to mount a desperate defense of the status quo.

At the very end of the 1980s, Gorbachev came closer to their point of view: he was also dismayed by the unruliness of the Soviet peripheries and the decline of central Soviet institutions. Gorbachev and the old-style nationalists, however, now had to do battle not just with each other but with the new ideologies and institutions that were emerging from the political ferment of the RSFSR. The new freedom of public association in the late 1980s had given rise to dozens of new political groupings. Gorbachev himself had sanctioned multi-candidate elections to the Congress of People's Deputies, the first even partially democratic parliament in Soviet history.

The nationalists were not oblivious to the need to give their efforts organized political reform. New Russophile groupings began to form in the spring of 1987. In the early days they tended to take as their primary rationale the defense of Russian culture and values in the face of the aggressive Westernization they saw in *perestroika*. The titles chosen for these organizations, including "The Association of Russian Artists" and "The Foundation of Slavic Writing and Cultures," reflected these priorities. In 1989, the most prominent nationalist spokesmen – who came almost exclusively from the class of privileged Soviet intellectuals – sought a broader social and political base by setting up organizations such as the United Workers' Front (which, despite its name, was never successful at recruiting the proletariat) and the United Council of Russia, which made its key goal the salvation of the USSR under the aegis of Slavic brotherhood.

Thus, in 1989, Soviet Russian nationalism turned decisively from the cultural domain to the political. It soon faced a searching examination of its credentials when its candidates ran for office in Soviet Russia's first free multiparty elections in the spring of 1990. It failed the test comprehensively. These Soviet Russian nationalists, so adept at operating in the closed Soviet world of patronage and subsidy, performed miserably in the new kind of electoral politics. Of sixty-one "patriotic" candidates in Moscow, not one reached the threshold of 50 percent needed to win at the first round of voting; only sixteen made it to the second round (which pitted the top two candidates from the first round against each other), and most of those were defeated.

The nationalists' failures at the ballot box, and their apparent inability to find a broader social base through open campaigning, led them to seek new allies and patrons. The only available candidates were the most unreconstructed "Red" conservatives in the Soviet establishment. Thus was sealed a tactical partnership between the "White" nationalists and the "Red" statists that was given organized political form by the emergence of a Russian Communist Party in the first half of 1990 (it was officially founded in June).

The belated arrival of this institution – just in time for the elimination of communism as a system of governance in Russia – pointed to the great weakness of the statist nationalists in 1990–91. They were left clutching at the political carapace of the USSR at a time when its body and soul were migrating elsewhere: to the emerging national institutions of the RSFSR. The only way they could begin to make themselves effective as political actors was to create an institution – a *Russian*, not *Soviet*, Communist Party – whose republican status contradicted the empire-saving logic of their political program.

In other words, the self-identifying "patriots" of late Soviet politics were continually hampered by their dependence on Soviet institutions and ways of thinking. Like their counterparts in Yugoslavia, who hoped to maintain power by substituting nationalism for their communism, Russian hard-liners played the nationalism card. Unlike the case of Yugoslavia, it did not work.

This was not primarily a matter of political incompetence, however. The differences between Russia and Serbia lay less in the political aptitude of the communists-turned-nationalists than in the context in which they operated. The Serbs were able to set themselves up against representatives of other proto-nations. The Russian nationalists had to compete for power with other Russians who were in fact no less nationalist than they – just nationalist in a different way. In 1990–91, the communist–nationalist bloc was outmaneuvered by the "democrats," who offered a version of nationalism more in tune with the times: instead of appealing relentlessly to Russia's mission as a great power and thousand years of strong statehood, it found at least some room for notions of popular sovereignty.

This was by no means an automatic development. Boris Yeltsin, who became the democrats' figurehead and prime mover in the middle of 1989, was a man nurtured by the Soviet system. He shot to prominence in the *perestroika* era because of his campaign against abuses in that same system: social justice was his cause, not nation-building. All this changed when Yeltsin gained a key position in the new politics of the RSFSR. As soon as he had secured the chairmanship of the Russian Congress of People's Deputies, he came out with the slogan of Russian sovereignty and expressed his determination to resist the "center." Here was the head of the Russian parliament applying national liberationist rhetoric on behalf of what many had believed to be an imperial people.

For the whole of 1990–91, the question of Russian nationhood was central to the very public feud between Yeltsin and Gorbachev. Nationalism served an invaluable tactical purpose in Yeltsin's struggle for power. A late convert to nationalism, Yeltsin was often vague and eclectic when it came to describing the precise extent of Russian statehood and the nature of Russian nationhood. But he was increasingly clear on two crucial points. First, the USSR should not be maintained in its present form if that required violence. In January 1991, Yeltsin clearly allied himself with the Baltic republics as they faced the threat of a coup by the Soviet military. Second, the building of a Russian nation was a matter of citizenship, not of ethnicity or of state power. In his inaugural address as Russian President in July 1991, Yeltsin placed the well-being of the people firmly above the goals of the state and struck an uncharacteristic self-deprecating note in describing his own role: "The president is not God, not a monarch, and not an omnipotent miracle worker; he is a citizen."[2]

This message clearly struck a chord with the citizens of the RSFSR. They voted convincingly for Yeltsin in the presidential elections, even though they had before them an alternative candidate (Vladimir Zhirinovsky) who stood unambiguously for ethnic and statist Russian nationalism. Surveys conducted in 1990–91 revealed a marked "de-imperialization" of Russian public opinion: more and more people came to believe that, if the preservation of the USSR in its present form could come only at the cost of coercion and strife, the game was not worth the candle.

But it is easy, with hindsight, to exaggerate the inevitability of the failure of "Red" nationalism in 1990–91. The balance of power between Soviet and Russian institutions was still unstable, as were the ideologies generated by those institutions. Russian politicians, like the electorates that brought them to power, did not have to make a firm choice between the USSR and Russia. Most people in the RSFSR approved the creation of their own parliament and presidency, but they also tended to consider themselves "Soviet" people first and foremost, and their underlying assumption was that the USSR would remain in existence (even if trimmed of the centrifugal Baltic states). In a referendum of March 1991, more than 70 percent of voters came out in favor of preserving the Soviet Union, but almost exactly the same number approved the creation of a popularly elected RSFSR presidency. The key question – the relationship between the emerging institutions of RSFSR statehood and the existing institutions of USSR statehood – was thus fudged by tens of millions of people. The wording of the key referendum question was itself vague enough to keep open all the hard questions regarding the true meaning of sovereignty: "Do you consider necessary the preservation of the Union of Soviet Socialist Republics as a renewed federation of equal sovereign republics, in which the rights and freedom of an individual of any nationality will be fully guaranteed?"[3]

By early 1991, a number of political groupings sought to resolve these ambiguities through the forceful imposition of Russian hegemony within Soviet political structures. Worrying signs of proto-fascism included the high public profile of radical nationalist groups, their efforts to incite violence in those parts of the "near abroad" that threatened to depart the union, and the rather high presidential vote for the demagogue Zhirinovsky (who came from nowhere to gain third place and 8 million votes). There were real grounds to fear that these right-wing extremists would make common cause with the empire-saving elite in the communist establishment.

This tense situation was resolved only after the crisis of the failed coup of August 1991, when a group of Soviet ministers and other high-ranking members of the establishment, desperate to shore up a collapsing state, attempted to take over a government they already notionally ran. In doing so, however, they brought about what they were desperate to avoid: they decisively discredited Soviet power, the Soviet Communist Party in particular, and the wider cause of empire-saving nationalism. In the months that followed, Russian

President Yeltsin was able to humiliate Soviet President Gorbachev and to take far-reaching decisions about the future status of Russia without consulting his electorate, let alone the Soviet party elite. In a rush of events at the start of December, Ukraine – by far the most important partner for any potential attempt to maintain the union – voted overwhelmingly for independence. A few days later, the leaders of the three Slavic republics unilaterally disbanded the Soviet Union.

This was a grand gesture, but it did little to determine the real meaning of the Russian nation. Russia, like the USSR, was a patchwork quilt of ethnicities; in the established Soviet term, it was a "multinational federation," which rather begged the question of how to envisage the overarching national unit. "Russia" could be defined in any one of a number of ways. It could be seen as a great power, as the successor state to the USSR. This approach had the advantage of continuity with the past and enjoyed a certain basic acceptance among the population, but it was certain to cause political tensions both nationally and internationally, and it was almost guaranteed to bring a sense of national humiliation: after all, the new Russia was much less powerful than the USSR had been. A second approach was to define the nation in ethnic terms: to present "Russia" as the state of all "Russians." In 1991 and 1992, however, this tactic, which would have roused rabbles or brought cohesion in other parts of Eastern Europe, had little prospect of succeeding on its own: partly because most "Russians" were more likely to see themselves as "Soviets," but also because an ethnic or cultural definition of nationality left dangling the 25 million "Russians" who lived in ex-Soviet states other than Russia. A third option was to see the nation in civic terms: to establish stable political institutions and the rule of law, and to extend membership in the Russian nation to all citizens governed by those institutions and subject to that law. A fourth was to define Russia in terms of what it was not: to play the anti-Western card.

These options were not mutually exclusive, and it is hard to see how they could possibly have been so: institutions, ideologies, and popular opinion were all in flux. In general, however, it would be fair to say that the early Yeltsin regime tended toward a civic definition of the nation in key areas of policy. After seventy years of single-party dictatorship, the mere fact of regular, free, and contested elections was a powerful nation-building statement: anyone with a vote – whatever their religion, skin color, or native language – was fundamentally "Russian." A further important signal was given by the liberal new law on citizenship adopted on November 28, 1991, which spoke of citizens of the Russian state (*rossiyanye*) rather than ethnic Russians (*russkiye*) and, unlike citizenship laws passed in other post-Soviet states, imposed no language requirement. The new law also extended generous provisions to potential citizens who were currently resident in other Soviet republics: such people were given until 2000 to move to the Russian Federation in order to claim automatic Russian citizenship.[4]

In the aftermath of the Soviet collapse, the Russian government treated the question of Russian populations in the "near abroad" (ex-USSR) with some restraint. The population of the Russian Federation, although in 1992–93 consistently expressing regret for the demise of the USSR, was not willing to act to restore it. Irredentist Russian nationalism in places like Estonia, Ukraine, and Kazakhstan was the dog that failed to bark in post-Soviet nationality politics. There were certainly tensions between Russians and the titular nationalities of new states, but (with the sole exception of Moldova) they did not lead to violent Russian intervention. The main reason for the absence of strife was that the Russian populations in the post-Soviet non-Russian nation-states did not speak with one voice. One survey of 1995–96, which polled ethnic Russians in Belarus, Ukraine, Moldova, Georgia, and Kazakhstan, found that only 13 percent of respondents identified themselves primarily as "Russian." A substantially greater number (23 percent) still thought of themselves as "Soviet," but 28 percent considered themselves simply citizens of the state they inhabited, and 20 percent identified with its titular nationality (Ukrainian, Moldovan, and so on).[5]

The absence of violence was a great blessing, but it did not necessarily provide a positive indication of a new kind of nationhood emerging in Russia. Soviet identity retained much of its resonance for citizens of the Russian Federation: in opinion polls, anywhere between 60 and 80 percent of ethnic Russians continued to consider the USSR, not Russia, to be their homeland.[6] Civic nationalism was thus a precarious ideology that was highly vulnerable to changes in political dynamics at both national and international levels. It faced a series of formidable challenges over the first couple of years of Russian independence. Yeltsin's professed hands-off policy with regard to Russians in the other post-Soviet states was tested by anti-Russian citizenship laws passed in Estonia and Latvia and by the failure to agree a dual citizenship arrangement with other parts of the former Soviet Union. By the mid-1990s Russia became less welcoming to migrants from the "near abroad," thus stepping back from the liberal position it had adopted at the end of 1991. Relations with other post-Soviet governments became increasingly bad-tempered as thorny issues – such as jurisdiction over Soviet military hardware and coordination of macroeconomic policy – came up for discussion. Worse still, the first post-Soviet parliamentary elections in December 1993 delivered a Duma dominated by neo-imperialist opinion that regularly expressed outrage at the plight of "compatriots" abroad and in March 1996 went so far as to revoke the decision made on December 12, 1991 by its predecessor, the Supreme Soviet, to ratify the Belovezh Forest Accords whereby the USSR was disbanded.[7] State policy at the highest level accordingly became more irascible and aggressive, entering a extended nationalist paroxysm whose most poisonous result was the invasion of Chechnya in December 1994.

All this did not mean, however, that national chauvinism had taken over Russian society. The first Chechen war was extremely unpopular; Russians were still not to be mobilized by ethnic hatred or by neo-imperialist *ressentiment*. What occurred in the mid-1990s was rather that politicians of various stripes attempted to find a nationalism that was effective in the confused conditions of post-Soviet Russia. Boris Yeltsin was not afraid to admit ignorance on this score: in the wake of his election victory in July 1996, he declared that the search was on for a new "Russian national idea." The ideas sent in by the general public were varied, but many recommended boosting state patriotism.[8] Yeltsin's problem, however, was that he was (with much justification) seen as a president who had removed all basis for patriotic pride by selling out to the oligarchs and reducing the state to a powerless and corrupt shadow of itself. When

Yeltsin did strike out in a statist direction – notably in the Chechen campaign – all he achieved was yet another humiliation for the Russian state.

Yeltsin, then, appeared vulnerable, and rival politicians queued up to take advantage. Foremost among them in the mid-1990s was Gennady Zyuganov, leader of the revamped Russian Communist Party, who campaigned in 1996 as the head of the Bloc of National-Patriotic Forces of Russia. Zyuganov had always been at the forefront of the coalition between nationalism and communism that took shape in 1990. He appealed to a sense of humiliated national pride, speaking regularly of the "genocide" that the "democrats" (always enclosed in venomous inverted commas in Zyuganov's writings) had inflicted on Soviet Russia. As he observed in one characteristic statement of conviction: "A great people – noble and generous in its greatness, charitable and forgiving from the heights of its power – is ridiculous and pitiful when it attempts to squeeze the boundless might bestowed on it by nature into the artificial borders of nationless, 'universal human' existence. This today is the fate of the Russian people."[9] As the 1990s wore on and the Sovietness of Russian identity began to fade, Zyuganov intensified the ethnic component of his rhetoric: a purportedly voluntary Slavic brotherhood would now stand in for the former imperial mission.

Zyuganov's overall message was undeniably appealing to a substantial part of the electorate. But there are reasons to doubt that his version of nationalism was central to his success. It seems most likely that more communist voters were casting their ballots in protest at economic reforms that had destroyed their well-being and sense of security. It is less clear that they had any stomach for what communist-style nationalism – if meant seriously – was likely to entail: prolonged and probably bloody conflict with ethnic and civic groups that did not stand to benefit from Zyuganov's vision. The same factor applied to an even greater extent in the case of Vladimir Zhirinovsky, whose national chauvinism attracted a substantial protest vote for its shock value, but no more than that. The most widely appealing nationalist vision put forward by a Russian politician in the middle of the 1990s was that of Alexander Lebed, the gravel-voiced hero of the Afghan war who was invited into government by

Yeltsin to help resolve the Chechen conflict. Lebed adopted a kind of folksy patriotism that did not underplay the military foundations of Russian nationhood but also urged a pragmatic and humane retreat from the "messianism" of Soviet imperialism. "Let's not dream of the happiness of mankind," he urged his compatriots, "let's sort out the happiness of our own country."[10]

Lebed's personal rating in advance of the 1996 presidential elections was the highest of all the candidates, although he came only a strong third on polling day. Under the terms of a pre-election pact, he lent his support to Yeltsin in the second round, thus ensuring the defeat of Zyuganov. Yet Lebed provided a useful pointer to a new kind of nationalism: statist but not imperialist, proudly patriotic but also pragmatic, orientated toward the army but also toward the Orthodox Church and the "creative genius" that Lebed ascribed to the Russian people. His vision chimed with that of many Russians in the late 1990s whose Sovietness was fading and who needed a compensatory Russianness, but were not willing to fish for that identity in the murky waters of neo-imperialism (even if most of them still could not quite understand why Ukraine needed to be a separate nation). This shift in values was reflected in a rise in the rate of declared Orthodox faith and in more secular expressions of national pride. Whereas in the first half of the 1990s Russian shoppers were mindful of the Soviet economic legacy and tended to assume that foreign goods were superior, toward the end of the decade they apparently were willing to believe that "home produce" was bound to be preferable. The phrase "Russian traditions of quality" would have provoked mirth in 1991 or even 1994, but in due course it entered the standard rhetorical arsenal of post-Soviet advertisers.

Yet the gradual reassertion of national pride also fed off a sense of isolation, vulnerability, and resentment. For the last two centuries, anti-Westernism has been a highly productive source of Russian national consciousness, and in the post-Soviet era it has once again proved its value. From 1994 onward, the Russian government tended to distance itself from Western states, viewing NATO expansion as an aggressive act. Government policy and popular opinion hardened further as a result of the bombing campaign against Serbia in 1999. Four years later, the Iraq war drove Russian attitudes toward "the West" in general, and the USA in particular, to a new post-Soviet low. More than 80 percent of Russians polled in the aftermath of the invasion viewed American actions "with disgust and indignation."[11]

The greatest stimulus to patriotic mobilization at the end of the 1990s came closer to home. In September 1999, the civilian population was terrorized by apartment bombings that were attributed to Chechen separatists. The Caucasus had indeed become a huge security risk to the Russian Federation as a consequence of the war launched by Boris Yeltsin five years earlier. Yeltsin's anointed successor, Vladimir Putin, renewed military action to overwhelming popular approval. In December 1999, the electoral success of the slickly promoted Unity movement confirmed that Russia's political landscape had been redrawn. Patriotism was no longer the preserve of communists and ex-Soviet neo-imperialists: it could now be professed by a younger, more pragmatic, de-ideologized generation of Russian politicians. The 2003 Duma elections results confirmed this analysis. The four parties that crossed the 5 percent threshold for proportional representation all claimed patriotism as a central tenet. The westernizing liberals – apparently so close to the seat of power in the early 1990s – were close to dropping off the electoral map entirely.

What exactly was the meaning of patriotism in Russian society under Putin? A 2004 survey found that World War II was firmly in first place as "the country's most significant achievement"; second place was taken by postwar reconstruction. Also prominent were the Russsian cultural heritage (as represented by great poets, writers, and composers) and Soviet–Russian achievements in sport and the space race. There was little evidence of nostalgia for prerevolutionary Russia; the October Revolution rated lower still as a positive point of reference. The clear leader in terms of nostalgia was the period dubbed "stagnation" by Gorbachev and his reformers: more than half of the over-forty-fives declared they would rather live in the Brezhnev period than in contemporary Russia.[12]

The most striking aspect of these survey results was how little had changed in people's values over the 1990s. Pride in the victory of 1945 had been a mainstay of mass consciousness for decades, and fondness for the perceived stability and social justice of the

1970s had emerged early in the post-Soviet era as a response to the social and psychological costs of market reform. But nostalgia for Soviet great power status and social order was not the only constituent in the emerging national identity. Russians were also increasingly inclined to identify themselves in ethnic terms. In a survey of 2004, 11.2 percent of respondents believed that Russia "should be a state of Russian people," and 34.2 percent that Russia was a multinational country but that Russians should have more rights than other groups. In other words, more than 45 percent of those polled believed that Russians should receive preferential treatment; just a few years earlier, in 1998, the equivalent figure had been in the region of 30 percent.[13] There were, moreover, reasons to fear that ethnic nationalism would boil up into racist violence at times of tension. The conflict in Chechnya was accompanied by heightened anti-Islamic feeling throughout Russia. In June 2002, almost one hundred years after an earlier instance of presumed racial superiority led Russia into a disastrous war in the Far East, a sporting defeat inflicted by an Asian nation was too much to bear for some spectators: central Moscow was hit by appalling riots after Russia's defeat by Japan in the football World Cup.

In addition, there were signs that the substantial de-imperialization of Russian attitudes that had occurred in the 1990s was grinding into reverse in the early twenty-first century. A telling test case was the public celebration of the sixtieth anniversary of the Soviet victory in World War II. In May 2005, more than fifty world leaders were due in Moscow to mark this occasion. The Estonians and the Lithuanians, however, stayed at home, resentful at Moscow's refusal to come to terms in any meaningful way with the legacy of Stalinism in the Baltics. It might seem a straightforward matter for the Putin administration to clear the air by distancing itself from annexations carried out sixty years previously. But the politics of apology came less naturally to Russian public figures than to their Anglo-American counterparts. What especially irked the Russians was the Estonian, Latvian, and Lithuanian contention that the Soviet government installed in 1945 was a regime of "occupation." They reiterated the official position: the Molotov–Ribbentrop pact of 1939, according to which Stalin and Hitler had carved up Eastern Europe between them, had been automatically canceled when Germany attacked the USSR in 1941; the annexationist secret protocols had in any case been publicly condemned by the Soviet Congress of People's Deputies in 1989, and there was no need to return to the question now. To a Western ear, these arguments sounded spurious and formalistic, but they reflected a reemerging patriotism combined with a sense of grievance that the Western allies continued to underestimate Russia's contribution in defeating Hitler and to downplay their own double standards (notably their failure to defend Czechoslovakia in 1938). Russian sensitivities were heightened by President Bush's itinerary on his trip to Eastern Europe for the victory celebrations: besides Moscow (where he presented himself as a Russophile), he visited Riga (where he was a Russophobe), and Georgia (where he was a valiant defender of an oppressed former colonial people).[14]

By the beginning of Putin's second term, the inculcation of patriotism became central to the regime's ideology. Russia's newest national holiday (June 12, the date of the declaration of RSFSR sovereignty in 1990) was celebrated with ever-increasing pomp and circumstance; in 2005 it was joined by a historically dubious National Unity Day (November 4, purportedly the date that Moscow was liberated from Polish occupation in 1612). In July 2005 the government announced a five-year plan to boost patriotism in Russian society that included the reintroduction in schools of military-style games and the provision of lessons in "correct reproductive behavior."[15]

Many readers' historical antennae may be set twitching by the mention of such aggressive state intervention in citizens' everyday lives: is this not a throwback to the age of Hitler, Mussolini, and Stalin? Such parallels would, however, overlook the fact that such intervention is the norm, not the fascist exception, in the early phases of nation-statehood that Russia is now experiencing.

Similarly, Russia lacks the potential for geopolitical mobilization on which fascism generally depends. Claims that Putin's Russia is virulently anti-Western and isolationist often seem exaggerated. Putin's declared mission is to bolster Russia's position as a world power, and he has proved a hard bargaining partner in negotiations with the EU. But he also sees himself emphatically as a *European*, not a Eurasian, leader; as a Western-style strong president, not as an "Eastern" despot. In 2001 he showed he was willing to take un-popular decisions to this effect when he gave his backing to US policy following 9/11. Even when we examine NATO expansion, the issue that has most consistently generated anti-Western feeling in Russian society over recent years, we find little militancy in either elite or popular attitudes – just a genuine pained perception of threat.[16] It also now seems to be the case that too many Russians – both in the political elite and in the sprawling middle class – have enjoyed the pleasures of international travel and foreign contacts for their anti-Westernism to grow from a tool of political rhetoric or a response to particular issues into an entire worldview.

It is true that statist patriotism is the new language of Russian poli-tics, and that politicians who do not speak it quickly find themselves marginalized. But that does not make Russia pathological or proto-fascist. National Communism – probably the most unpalatable and politically dangerous patriotic movement of the 1990s – has started to look ideologically bankrupt as its Soviet restorationist ideology becomes anachronistic. The patriotism served up by the president and his many allies in the Duma is more upbeat, and less infused with post-imperial resentment, than seemed likely in the mid-1990s. Certainly, Putin's nationalism is vague and evasive. In his speeches he constantly alludes to the legacy of Soviet greatness without ex-ploring the precise implications of that legacy in the politics of the present; he also downplays or distorts the problems that his version of patriotism has failed to solve (notably Chechnya). The vagueness and the evasions play well with a public that continues to feel more than a twinge of regret for the collapse of Soviet statehood and that prefers not to be reminded of the complex human tragedy still un-folding in the deep south of the Russian Federation. In comparison with its predecessors, Russian nationalism in the Putin era is bland and ideologically inexplicit. What it does show in abundance is a commitment to create and maintain a strong, proud, geopolitically robust, "modern," prosperous state. But there is nothing remarkable in that: "stateness" has been overwhelmingly the most important component of nationhood in the modern world – especially in parts of that world that have conspicuously lacked such stateness until the very recent past.

More worthy of note is the mere fact that Russia has come to acquire an effective statist nationalism after floundering throughout the 1990s in search of this attribute. Nation-building in post-Soviet Russia was always certain to be a vexed undertaking. Here was a purportedly imperial people (the Russians) that declared itself to be suffering the pangs of (Soviet) decolonization. It is as if Britain in the late 1940s had put itself in the same category as India, claiming to be undergoing the identical process of troubled liberation from empire. Perhaps the closest historical parallel is the emergence of Turkey from the ruins of the Ottoman Empire, though Turkish nation-building was catalyzed by military defeat in a way that Russia's was not, and Atatürk was able to operate in a one-party state rather than the fractious proto-democracy that Yeltsin inhabited.

The scene was set for politicians in Russia to gamble on nationalism to gain whatever tactical advantage they could. Xenophobic and neo-imperialist versions of nationalism seemed to have every chance of success. The Russian case conformed fully to one of the iron laws of post-communism: in conditions of radical uncertainty over political institutions, social justice, and even state boundaries, *all* politicians try to use nationalism in their interests. Some find that the nationalism card gives them a winning hand; others do not. This game was played in Russia throughout the 1990s, but it had no conclusive winner. Boris Yeltsin remained in power, but his legitimacy tailed off rapidly and his vision of nationalism vacillated between a civic model that was frequently contradicted in practice and a statist model that was undermined by the palpable weakness of the Yeltsinite state. Yeltsin's main rivals for power, the new "patriotic" communists, had a more coherent and unequivocal vision of the Russian nation, but it was always likely to divide Russian society as much as it united it, and the plausibility of any form of communism was bound to weaken as the Soviet Union retreated further into history.

National identity was a muddle in post-Soviet Russia, which was almost certainly a good thing: its vagueness obscured the road to power for authoritarian demagogues who in other circumstances would surely have profited from the traumatic uncertainty and impoverishment faced by the Russian population in the 1990s. Under

Putin, however, a widely accepted national patriotism seems to have taken shape. This development was made possible partly by the mere passing of time. As the hardship and political struggles of the 1980s faded in people's minds, fond memories of Soviet military victory or of the social contract of the Brezhnev era could now be mobilized as part of an emphatically post-Soviet national identity without raising the prospect of imperial revanche. The "patriotic" Communist Party, the main political force that preyed on feelings of national humiliation arising from the Soviet collapse, was comprehensively outmaneuvered by a new political party (Unity) and a new president (Putin) whose ideology was patriotic without being neo-Soviet. Liberalism, communism's ideological antagonist throughout the 1990s, was tainted by the shenanigans of the Yeltsin era and put up no serious resistance. All these, however, were enabling factors for the emergence of a new nationalism. The short-term catalyst, as so often in the history of modern nationalism, was war. Russia's newly found patriotic unity required a mobilizing cause and a foe: the North Caucasus, as explained in the final chapter of this book, provided both of these.

5 | A free market?

There was no more challenging area of post-communist transformation than the economy. Although Soviet people might be amazed or shocked by the precipitate decline of the USSR and the equally rapid emergence of Yeltsinite Russia, they did at least grasp what was occurring. Decades of living under a regime that talked politics incessantly had given them tools to make sense of what they saw and read, even if it appalled them. They had a healthy disrespect for politicians combined with a sense of the possible outcomes of political reforms: free elections, a parliament, parties, perhaps a democratically elected president. In the economic sphere, by contrast, it is far less obvious that Russians were prepared for what was about to hit them. The problem was not that people were in the main hostile to the idea of some kind of market. From 1987 onwards, decades of ineffectual grumbling about the inadequacies of the economic system crescendoed to a sustained growl of pain and anger as shortages reached epidemic proportions. By 1991, there was an overpowering sense that something radical needed to be done, and "market reform" seemed to many to fit the bill.

How exactly was a viable market to be achieved on Soviet economic foundations? Here the problems were immense. The Soviet system lacked the most basic prerequisites of a market economy. There was no private ownership of the means of production, which made it unclear who the agents of a market economy might be and how the incentives for market activity might be created. Money was not properly convertible internally, let alone in the international financial arena. Although the ruble was the nominal Soviet currency, many large transactions between enterprises were carried out in "virtual" money: the so-called "non-cash" rubles that had meaning only in the context of byzantine Soviet accounting procedures. Prices in the official economy were strictly controlled, which led to overproduction and shortages. The deficiencies of the system were only partially alleviated by an unofficial economy where prices were, by contrast, artificially high. The Soviet system lacked the infrastructure of a market economy: stock markets, insurance companies, accountancy firms, commercial law. Banks did exist, but they were little more than the current accounts of branches of the Soviet state. In the USSR, economics was entirely at the service of politics. Enterprises were kept afloat not because they met any form of market demand, but because they occupied a niche in the military–industrial complex that had been synonymous with Soviet statecraft since the 1930s.

All this was bad enough, but there was worse for would-be reformers in post-Soviet Russia. The condition of the Soviet economy, already weak in its fundamentals, had taken a sharp downward turn as a result of Mikhail Gorbachev's reforms. Gorbachev and his advisors were acutely aware of the inefficiency and wastefulness of the Soviet economy, and of its unfriendliness to the consumer. They aimed to revitalize economic life by giving Soviet citizens a new sense of purpose: by offering the incentives that would turn people into energetic and responsible economic actors. The first step in this direction was a 1987 law on "individual labor activity" that began to make more respectable the notion of entrepreneurship, though entrepreneurs were still prohibited from using anyone's labor but their own. The next, more permissive, legislative moves were a law on state enterprises (January 1988), which allowed individual enterprises to make their own production decisions, keep their own profits, and set their own wage levels, and a law on cooperatives (May 1988) that enabled people to set up de facto small businesses using assets and infrastructure owned by Soviet organizations. The legislators' intention was that the cooperatives would quickly start to provide the consumer goods and services that the Soviet command economy had so tangibly neglected. The new laws met a lively response from the population. The number of cooperatives grew from 14,000 on January 1, 1988 to 77,500 at the start of the following year. Official figures for 1991 gave a figure of 135,000 registered cooperatives that produced nearly 3 percent of all consumer goods and an impressive 18.4 percent of services.[1]

On paper, the Gorbachev reforms might appear to be sensible

gradualist measures. In practice, however, they had serious short-comings. The regulations still gave bureaucrats ample scope to obstruct new business ventures, which meant that successful cooperatives were often those whose proprietors enjoyed the right contacts. This was far from being a free and open business culture. Its less favored participants had to face constant bureaucratic obstruction as well as increasing menace from racketeers. Its well-connected beneficiaries had every businessman's dream: the freedom to make good profits from a shortage economy where just about any consumer item was bound to meet intense demand, but without the responsibility of legal ownership or the need to come up with start-up capital. It was in the cooperative movement of the late 1980s that the future oligarch Mikhail Khodorkovsky gained the initial funds that he would put to more lucrative uses in the mid-1990s. Managers of larger non-cooperative enterprises also enjoyed a much freer hand than hitherto: they were able to speculate on the rudimentary commodity markets of the late Soviet period and to raise their workers' wages in the knowledge that the state would have to bail them out if they ran at a loss.

Another, even more fundamental, problem with the economic policy of *perestroika* was that Gorbachev remained unashamedly a one-party state socialist for whom the boundary between legitimate market activity and illegitimate "profiteering" was friable – and liable to disappear entirely at moments of political stress. Sure enough, Gorbachev tried several times to rein in the cooperative movement after he had set it in motion. He also, in 1990–91, tended increasingly to side with political and economic conservatives as he saw the basis of his own power as Soviet president crumbling away. He eventually pushed aside programs for rapid economic transformation and instead sanctioned rises in social benefits without removing caps on pricing. The result was a colossal amount of concealed inflation. A ton of crude oil fetched 30 rubles in the official system of Soviet wholesale trade; on the unofficial market, that amount of money could buy precisely one packet of Marlboro cigarettes.[2] The state was printing money to hide the decline in marketable production, and the budget deficit probably (the dire state of Soviet statistics does not permit certainty) swelled to a near-catastrophic 30 percent of GDP. Worst of all, as the newly autonomous enterprises sucked goods out of the state sector, the Soviet population was enduring the most desperate shortages it could remember for decades. By autumn 1991, as I myself witnessed in Yaroslavl, people sometimes had to queue two nights in a row just to buy milk.

As Gorbachev's power base shrank, a new political regime with a different economic strategy gained in strength. Boris Yeltsin was a man with plenty of old-style Soviet authoritarian and paternalist instincts, but he also enjoyed taking decisive measures, sensed the need for drastic action to avert economic meltdown, and was delighted to use economic reform as yet another weapon in his power struggle with the Soviet president. In December 1990, he passed new laws on enterprises and on property, and by the autumn of 1991 he had moved a number of young market-orientated economic reformers to positions where they could make an impact.

Here, then, is the starting point for post-Soviet economic reform and a base-line for adjudicating what remains in Russia the most controversial question of the "transition" era: should the market reformers be regarded as pioneers and heroes or as villains and crooks? Were they supremely energetic visionaries or highly competent technocrats or out-of-touch blunderers or hard-hearted ideologues or cynical influence-peddlers? When Anatoly Chubais, the most instantly recognizable and politically long-lived of the original 1991 reform team, reached his fiftieth birthday in 2005, his sympathizers wished him a long life and a less hostile country on which to work his wonders. His opponents clearly saw him as little better than a state criminal: "Fifty years, and still at liberty?" asked the leader of a patriotic grouping in the Duma with mock incredulity.[3] Much commentary on the economic reforms has a Manichaean quality: either market crusaders do battle with retrograde apparatchiks and "Red" enterprise directors, or decent hard-working Soviet people are fleeced by corrupt *biznesmeny* with the cynical connivance of anticommunist economic reformers who took their orders from Harvard, not from the Russian electorate.

To begin to adjudicate between these violently conflicting interpretations, we need to return to 1991–92 and examine both the problems identified by the reformers and the solutions they came up with. The challenge, as Chubais and his comrades saw it, was to wrench Russia out of its economic vortex of increased government spending and plummeting production by setting up the right conditions for market activity. That meant taking the state out of economic life in as many ways as possible. The most basic task was to make money meaningful by eliminating state controls over pricing. Liberalization of prices for many commodities was instigated by deputy prime minister Yegor Gaidar and duly implemented on January 2, 1992. It undeniably made an impact. Within weeks the shelves of Russian shops were better stocked, and money, for the first time in seven decades, seemed to be doing its job of accurately reflecting value. Of course, prices were now out of many people's reach, and galloping inflation (more than 2,500 percent in 1992 alone) wiped out personal savings in a matter of weeks. By the reformers' lights, however, this was a necessary consequence of reform: better to dynamize the economy than to honor the debased Soviet rubles languishing in unproductive savings accounts.

The other task the reformers set themselves was to relinquish state ownership. They worked on the assumption that Russians were no less rational economic actors than people in the West: if provided with the right incentives – in the first instance secure ownership of assets – they would become law-abiding but dynamic and risk-taking capitalists and would elbow aside the hundreds of thousands of monopoly-abusing apparatchiks that Russia already possessed. But the task of privatization was a daunting one. Not only was it necessary to draw up rules that would work for the many different sectors of a vast economy, it was also necessary to create the concept of "ownership" from scratch: to convince the population that the state would honor the property rights it was now dispensing, and to induce or coerce office-holders not to obstruct the exercise of these rights.

The state retained ownership of all land and of politically sensitive industries such as oil and gas, medical supplies, and weapons production. Most other assets, however, it was in principle willing to sign away into private ownership. The least controversial, though not necessarily the simplest, form of privatization was that of individual or family housing: this was sanctioned in the late Soviet era and vigorously encouraged from 1992 onward. In Moscow, the vanguard of economic activity, 365,584 apartments had been privatized by the end of 1992, and about a quarter of the total housing stock by September 1993.[4] In other places privatization also made headway in the first two years of post-communism, though it proceeded by fits and starts, as municipal authorities, enterprises, and individual citizens advanced their often conflicting claims on property. By early 1995, about a third of apartments in Russia (11 million) had been privatized.[5]

A second tier of privatization was that of small businesses, primarily in the retail and service industries. This kind of transition of ownership had been occurring de facto since the late 1980s in the cooperative movement and by 1992 had acquired enormous momentum. By the middle of the decade, privatized small businesses numbered in the hundreds of thousands – though they labored under the double burden of obstructive bureaucracy and organized crime.

The third tier of privatization, and the one that mainly preoccupied the reformers, was that of medium-sized and large enterprises: everything from biscuit factories and breweries to steel mills and mines. Such enterprises, though they formally remained in state ownership until the privatization campaign of 1993–94, already had their own proprietors: the industrial managers who knew the ropes of the late Soviet economy better than anyone and controlled the resources of their enterprises to a more absolute extent than their managing director counterparts in the West. The reformers' preference was to weaken the control of the Soviet bosses through the privatization process by ensuring that "insiders" (the workers and management at a given enterprise) would not receive a controlling stake. In the end, given the powerful lobby that industrial interests formed in the Congress of People's Deputies, they had to settle for a compromise: in most newly privatized companies, "insiders" would be allotted 51 percent of the shares.

Both at the time and afterwards, the reform team argued that this minor concession was much less significant than the astonishing speed and thoroughness with which the first phase of privatization was conducted. Between the end of 1992 and the middle of 1994, enterprises were sold at hundreds of auctions in all parts of Russia. By July 1994, more than 15,000 large and mid-sized companies, with a total of about 17 million employees, had been privatized. A further eighteen months later, at the start of 1996, 88.3 percent of Russia's industrial workers were employed in privatized enterprises.[6] A further feather in the reformers' cap was that millions of "ordinary" people had been made stakeholders in the economy. In October 1992, all citizens were granted a voucher to the face value of 10,000 rubles (about $40 at the time) with which they could acquire shares in the privatized companies. More than 40 million people took advantage of the opportunity, which made 28 percent of the Russian population shareholders in their national economy (compared with a mere 20 percent in the USA).[7]

By the middle of 1994, Russia could claim to have completed a privatization programme beyond the wildest dreams even of Margaret Thatcher. The reformers could also congratulate themselves on the obvious signs of entrepreneurial vigor in Russian society. Hundreds of thousands of new small businesses had been set up. Street trading, only explicitly legalized by a presidential decree of January 29, 1992, had now taken over Russia's cities. In Russia just about everything could be, and was, bought and sold. Even contract killing had a well-established going rate: $7,000 in 1995 for the assassination of a man without a bodyguard.[8] The institutions of capitalism were appearing. Russia could now boast two thousand or so private banks, and foreign investment was surging as international confidence in the Russian market grew. Anders Åslund, a Swedish diplomat who worked as an economic advisor to the Russian government between November 1991 and January 1994, was able to claim that by the end of 1993 Russia had indeed become a market economy, in the sense that the market was now the main means of allocation of goods.[9] The Russians had proved wrong the complacent Western observers who reckoned that "Muscovite" political traditions had knocked the entrepeneurial nous out of them.

Admittedly, this market economy made some observers blanch – and not only those of a socialist persuasion. The liberalizing reforms had released the currency from Soviet price controls, but they had failed to get it back under control: to hold down inflation. What this meant was that the less affluent or well-connected members of society were heavily penalized: unable to find any profitable home for their money, they saw it plummet in value. Inflation was a draconian tax on the poor. It was also a powerful disincentive for the emerging business class to engage in "normal" capitalist practices. When banks could deliver quick and constant profits through currency speculation, it was economic folly for them to tie money up in longer-term investments. In early 1992, a resourceful novice entrepreneur could make $2 million in seventy-two hours simply by arranging for a wealthy client the transfer to a Western bank account the ruble equivalent of $20 million.[10] Loopholes were everywhere in the post-Soviet economy. Because prices for key commodities – notably energy – continued to be internally regulated, anyone with access to an international market where prices were often ten times higher had a license to print money. To make matters worse, a large and growing sector of the economy did not even pretend to be playing by the rules. Organized crime had taken an apparently unshakable grip on substantial sectors of the business world. According to statistics produced by the Ministry of Internal Affairs, the growth rate for cases of extortion was anything from 15 to 30 percent each year between 1990 and 1996.[11]

Even in the privatization programme – the pride and joy of the reformers – all was not quite as it seemed. Many Russians cashed in their vouchers almost as soon as they acquired them in the late autumn of 1992. The figure of 40 million shareholders at the end of the privatization campaign in mid-1994 needs to be compared with the more than 140 million Russians who were able to claim their vouchers at branches of the Sberbank (national savings bank). The old enterprise directors often proved adept at acquiring the shareholdings of their workforce. Employees might be forced to part with their shares either for nothing or at knock-down prices if they resigned their job or were fired. Alternatively, directors might offer incentives to sell – either by offering ready cash when share prices were still low or by using company funds to buy consumer goods to offer in exchange for shares. Another option was simply to defraud the shareholding workforce. Directors were also intent on keeping out or sidelining outsiders. They diluted other parties' shareholdings through impromptu share issues, kept major shareholders off the board, or forgot to invite them to meetings. Enterprises also starved potential investors of the information they needed to gauge the strength of the company. Shareholder registers were kept secret. Worse still, there was often no open market in shares. Potential investors, if they did not have the necessary insider contacts, almost literally had to go to the factory gates and buy shares from the employees as they left work. The result was that, by the mid-1990s, no more than a fifth of enterprises were outsider-controlled. Cases of enterprises saved by enlightened Swedish or German investment and know-how did occur – they included for example the St. Petersburg brewery Baltika – but they were a small minority. Many enterprise directors were managing director and board of shareholders rolled into one: hardly a recipe for capitalist accountability.

In their more candid moments, the economic reformers admitted the economy they had brought into being was far from perfect. But they had no shortage of people and circumstances to blame for its shortcomings. The main problem was that they were not conducting the reform in a political vacuum but in the face of fierce resistance from communist and nationalist groups in parliament and from powerful interest groups who straddled politics and the economy: the "Red directors" and the apparatchiks. The reformers never built a secure political base of their own, and they received a severe setback in the December 1993 elections, which delivered an obstreperous anti-reform Duma. As a result, economic policy fluctuated between free market orthodoxy and protectionism. Even Boris Yeltsin had a tendency to revert to Soviet-style economic management. When confronted by angry babushkas in Nizhnii Novgorod one week after price liberalization in January 1992, his response was to decree a price reduction on the spot – thus flatly contradicting the policy that was supposedly the cornerstone of his economic strategy at that point.[12] The strict monetary policy that Gaidar wished to follow in 1992 and 1993 did not turn out to be a realistic option, since the Central Bank, which he could not control, continued to churn out rubles and cheap credits for failing enterprises. Until the middle of 1993, moreover, Russia remained economically locked into the Commonwealth of Independent States, which allowed the other former Soviet republics to funnel low-priced Russian exports to foreign markets. As for the criminalization of the economy, the reformers could argue that this was the unavoidable legacy of the Soviet informal economy and of the weakness of the law in Russia.

Perhaps the most powerful argument that the reformers could mount in their defense was that in 1994 or 1995 it was simply too early to judge them. A transformation as massive and complex as this was bound to be messy and to have painful and undesirable side-effects; the key question was whether, or how quickly, they would wear off. Chubais and Gaidar were placing their bets on a new class of capitalist investors emerging from the chaos of voucher privatization with substantial consolidated shareholdings which they would start to trade on an open and competitive stock market. They looked on with approval as the Russian-speaking American banker Boris Jordan, through a combination of good contacts and sheer legwork, acquired a total of 17 million vouchers, which he then used to buy stakes in Russian companies on behalf of his Western clients. A further encouraging sign was the arrival of a Russian stock market, which from September 1994 had a computerized trading system. Admittedly, trading was monopolized by a small group of brokers in Moscow and a few other cities, and it allowed no space for the small investor. But perhaps that would come with time.

From 1995 onwards, some new measures were taken to "normalize" the economy. The banks found that the outrageous profits of the early 1990s were no longer available, as the government finally brought inflation under control for a sustained period. What the government took away with one hand, however, it gave back with the other. Chronically short of money, unable to extract taxes from society, and unwilling to stoke inflation by printing its own money, the state filled the holes in its own budget by selling promissory notes (known as GKOs): in other words, by raising loans from the very same bankers and company owners it had done so much to enrich in the first half of the decade. The lenders – mainly the banks – were delighted to oblige, since their profits from other sources had started to dry up, and the state, for all its failings, was as reliable a debtor as you were likely to find in post-Soviet Russia.

Here the government was bailing itself out of economic difficulties by selling its debts on the open market. A far more egregious arrangement with finance capitalists was made late in 1995, when the Yeltsin regime effectively sold a substantial portion of its largest and most lucrative companies to a group of tycoons in exchange for the powerful support they could offer the incumbent president at a politically and economically vulnerable stage of his reign. The second wave of privatization, announced in 1994 and implemented in 1995, had gone badly, and the government was short of cash. It still had an enormous number of assets that could be made liquid: controlling stakes in Russia's largest corporations and full ownership of numerous companies in sectors like gas, oil, and metals. In November and December 1995, a dozen of these crown jewels of the Russian economy were auctioned off as collateral for massive bank loans on which the government was bound to default. Foreign investors and all other outsiders were kept out of the bidding. One insider, Vladimir Potanin, paid just over $170 million for a 38 percent stake in Norilsk Nickel, a company whose reported profits in 1995 were $1.2 billion.[13] The "loans-for-shares" scheme, as it quickly became known, was simply the most outrageous case of insider dealing in history. By 1997, seven men (the "oligarchs") were reckoned to control 50 percent of the Russian economy.

It is not self-evident why even a state as poor and demoralized as Russia in the mid-1990s would acquiesce in what some have called a Faustian bargain with Boris Berezovsky, Mikhail Khodorkovsky, and other moguls of dubious rectitude. One factor undeniably was the sheer chutzpah of the oligarchs in proposing such a scheme in the first place – not to mention their determined and unscrupulous advocacy. But Chubais and other key government figures who saw the scheme exactly for what it was were swayed by the adrenalin of political combat, by the power of free market ideology, and by the conviction that a return of communism must be avoided at all costs. Russia, in their view, had to avoid the common Eastern European scenario of the 1990s according to which economic liberals were felled by protest votes against the social depredations brought on by their policies. Like their predecessors in the first Russian Revolution, they believed that the ends justified the means, that a political setback for them would be an unmitigated disaster for everyone, and that democracy and progress were a zero-sum game at least for the medium term.

Whatever the undesirable political consequences of the hegemony of the oligarchs – the gross devaluation of the concept and practice of democracy in Russia, the state's loss of any lingering credibility it possessed as the upholder of the law – it did not do Russia's economy any harm in the short term. Foreign investors, some of them severely stung earlier in the decade, came back for more. In 1997, the Russian stock market could claim to be "the most profitable emerging market in the world."[14] But the next crash was not long in coming. In 1998, the Russian economy, already undermined by the weakness of the state that underwrote it, was infected by the "Asian flu" that had swept the Far East and undermined international business confidence. On August 17 the Russian government bowed to overpowering market pressure, abandoned its efforts to keep the ruble in a stable band, devalued its currency, and defaulted on its debts. The most prominent casualties of the crisis were the commercial banks, which had acquired foreign currency debts that were now ruinously expensive to service and had overinvested in government promissory notes that were now worthless pieces of paper.

In a broader perspective, however, the Russian economy did not take long to bounce back from its latest setback. Rising oil prices in the late 1990s were one boon to Russia's key industries. Another was the weak ruble, which suddenly made Russian products highly competitive on the world market. The result was a steady growth rate that continued well into the Putin era (though it began to slow in 2004). It might appear, therefore, that the Russian market economy was already, within fifteen years of the collapse of Soviet economic institutions, in a robust state. The fact is, however, that short-term trends do not prove anything much. A more rewarding exercise is to inquire how exactly this economy worked on the ground.

Post-Soviet Russia had many of the trappings of capitalism but much less of its essence. Foreign visitors and Russian reformers alike were impressed by the rapid emergence of hundreds of new banks in the early 1990s, many of them with smart Moscow offices staffed by immaculately besuited personnel. On closer inspection, however, these institutions did not do many of the things people expect banks to do in the West: they did not offer mortgages and had very little to do with "ordinary" investors. The loans they made were overwhelmingly short-term. A survey of Moscow banks in early 1997 revealed that only 1.2 percent of a total $20 billion currently loaned by Moscow banks was for longer than one year.[15] Instead of maintaining financial independence, many banks even in the Putin era were closely tied to the organizations that had originally set them up and remained resistant to regulation and transparency.[16] Poorly integrated into world financial markets, they were effectively the financial wings of the various business empires that formed in the 1990s. The main source of their money was not market activity per se but rather the links to government that allowed them to find loopholes or successfully second-guess the economy at minimal risk to themselves (until, in August 1998, the state finally let them down). Because they were not good at securing investment, Russian banks remained small by global standards. In 1997, 60 percent of them had under $1 million in capital.[17]

It is hard, however, to hold the banks primarily responsible for their own short-termism. The Russian economy in the 1990s lacked many of the support institutions that make a market economy tick. If people are to become rational market actors – by engaging freely in profit-maximizing transactions – they need to be reasonably confident that the other parties in these transactions will prove reliable, or, if not, that they hold some guarantees against unreliability. This kind of concern is bound to be especially acute in an economy undergoing transformation: how were post-Soviet Russians to be sure that their business partners would not exploit their newly granted economic freedom by fleecing them?

In a well-established market economy business people try to minimize risk by making themselves maximally well-informed about their potential transaction partners. They can ask around, they can run credit checks, they can consult the stock market, they can examine publicly available financial records. If a transaction still goes wrong, the law provides a useful backstop.

Post-Soviet Russia lacked most of these risk-minimizing institutions. The insurance market was almost non-existent. Accurate assessments of the financial robustness of business partners were difficult if not impossible. Relatively few companies were listed on the stock exchange. Corporate governance was lax and financial records were scanty. The legal system was perceived to be cumbersome, corrupt, and ineffectual. And post-Soviet life served up numerous reminders of how disastrously unreliable and unpredictable the market could be. The most notorious case occurred in the spring and summer of 1993, when a businessman named Sergei Mavrodi persuaded millions of people to invest in a company, MMM, that had only been authorized to sell 991,000 shares. When this classic pyramid scheme collapsed in July 1993, investors were left without any recourse to the law – and the instigator of the scam avoided prosecution.[18]

Most aspects of post-Soviet economic life can be understood better if they are seen as a response to the chronic risk and uncertainty of the times. Instead of seeking out the most profitable deal on an open market, people tended to go with partners they knew and could trust. Instead of breaking up into smaller and more profitable economic units, major industrial enterprises – the dinosaurs of the Soviet economy – gathered together in ever more elaborate trading conglomerates: their solution to the risk of the market was never to do business "outside the family." Banks and credit agencies would lend only to people they had strong first-hand reasons to trust. Russian credit card providers in the 1990s did not use a formal system of credit scoring to decide on their customers. AmEx, for example, selected its customers from applicants personally recommended by its own employees. Although banks were willing to consider friends of friends of employees as well as personal acquaintances, they tended to keep the degree of separation within limits: an application would look dubious if there was more than one person in the chain of connection between potential client and bank official. In any case, a face-to-face interview with the applicant was considered essential – and much more important than any form-filling exercises.[19]

Reduction of uncertainty can be seen to lie at the root even of the ugliest and most notorious phenomenon of Russian *kapitalizm*: the mafia. Organized crime attracted a good deal of attention in the 1990s, not least because it permeated the areas of Russian life with which Western visitors were likely to be most familiar: shops, hotels, and restaurants in the major cities. Very few people had an interest in understating the extent of the mafia: economic reformers needed a scapegoat, opposition politicians needed to condemn Yeltsin's crony capitalism, journalists needed good copy, and criminals themselves thrived on sensationalist publicity because it persuaded businesses to accept them as a fact of life.[20] Just as in the Western press burglars tend to get much more attention than the corporate insider dealers whose crimes against property are immeasurably greater, so the gangland shootings of post-Soviet Russia received more public exposure than the routine abuses that enabled a group of a few tens of thousands of capitalists to appropriate tens of billions of dollars from the Russian state.

Such distortions of perspective make it imperative for us to be clear what we are talking about when we use the word "mafia." This was not a single umbrella organization masterminding organized crime across the whole of Russia. "Mafias" were for the most part highly localized and often had some clear ethnic or regional identity. Often unsophisticated in their operations, they made money by carrying out numerous small-time deals or by controlling access to certain markets. They collected protection money, "tribute," from shops and other small businesses. Or they engaged profitably in illicit trade by organizing the removal of goods and raw materials from enterprises and then striking deals with border officials to cash in on the export of these commodities to the lucrative foreign market.

There can be no doubt that economic activity in post-Soviet Russia was accompanied by plenty of fraud, extortion, and violent crime. Instead of condemning such activities out of hand, however, we should reflect on what made them possible. The main reason was the headlong withdrawal of the state from enforcement of legal titles and contracts. The reformers in government had handed out property rights at a speed without precedent, but without providing any effective means of defending those rights. It had thereby created a ferocious (but not at all "free") market in the enforcement of property rights.[21] "Violent entrepreneurs" (a more neutral phrase than "mafia") can thus be said to have compensated for the inadequacies of the state: to have "privatized" the violence over which less dysfunctional states hold a legitimate monopoly. Organized crime was almost certainly less of a hindrance overall to business operations than the interference of an arbitrary and corrupt state bureaucracy. In a 1996 survey, more than 40 percent of shop owners polled in Moscow, Smolensk, and Ulyanovsk admitted they had dealings with "racketeers," but they also rated them a less severe problem than taxes and lack of investment.[22]

The post-Soviet "mafia" should thus be seen not as the primary causes of economic underperformance and moral degradation but as a kind of brutal economic facilitator that takes over the law-enforcing functions abandoned by the state. But, if organized crime is a solution of sorts to a deficit in legal culture, it is far from being a good solution. It is inequitable and demoralizing, of course, but it is also much less efficient than the free market mechanisms for which it substitutes. In the clinical language of economics, it involves high "transaction costs." Commodities take far longer to travel from their producers to their consumers than they would in a more transparent system, and acquire large but arbitrary mark-ups on the way. In bypassing the open market, moreover, non-state contract enforcement, like corruption, pushes further into the future the time when the legal system might be recognized as an arbiter in economic disputes.

Musclemen in the mafia groupings and corrupt officials in the state bureaucracy are symptoms of a much deeper problem: Russia became a market economy in the 1990s, but this was by no means a free market. It offered incentives not for clear-sighted business strategy but for ad hoc insider dealing. It is hard otherwise to explain why rates of new entrepreneurship declined at precisely the moment you would expect them to increase: when the currency was stabilized in the mid-1990s and a "normal" business environment seemed to be taking shape.

A profound consequence of this incentive structure was that the economy in the second half of the 1990s changed much less in its fundamentals than the architects of privatization had assumed it would. The major industrial enterprises were not, for the most part, transformed into dynamic market actors. Their resistance to change was partly due to the continued reign of "Red directors" who were able to strike deals with local political elites and to keep out the outside investors who might have brought financial salvation, but who would also have undermined the incumbent bosses' authority. But the main reason why many medium-sized and large Russian enterprises did not adapt in the ways that the reformers had intended was that they would have been ruined if they had done so. Perhaps as many as half of them were not viable on the open world market, and the paucity of sources of domestic investment meant they could not generate quick capital to undertake any radical overhaul.

To make matters even worse, they were squeezed by a state that was running desperately short of cash. Government at various levels undertook massive cutbacks in expenditure – thus substantially withdrawing the generous credits that underperforming enterprises had formerly enjoyed – and a feverish bout of new tax legislation. Tens of thousands of decrees, laws, and other normative proclamations were issued: nearly 50,000 federal government instructions in 1993 alone.[23] A presidential decree of December 1993 allowed local government to levy up to eighteen taxes of its own.[24] But the Russian experience in the 1990s showed that the correlation between sheer legislative activity and effective rule of law is weak (if not inverse). Many entrepreneurs discovered that, if they played by all the rules all the time, they would pay well over 100 percent of their profits in taxes. The Russian state had not grasped the elementary truth that to demand taxes is not the same thing as to receive them.

Given this unfavorable economic environment, it is not surprising that the proportion of loss-making enterprises was stable through the 1990s at about 40 percent, whatever the highs and lows of world oil prices.[25] What requires explanation is how these enterprises kept going in spite of everything. Their first expedient, in the absence of government support, was to shrink. Industrial production fell by 40 percent between 1991 and the end of 1993. A tenth of the workforce was cut in 1992–93.[26] Those workers who remained on the books often had to wait months to be paid, and the social services that their enterprises had formerly dispensed – housing, childcare, holidays – were cut back.

An even more effective way of cutting costs was not paying taxes. Some sectors of the economy – notably the gigantic energy company Gazprom – had friends in high places and were able to lobby successfully for enormous tax breaks (which in 1994 probably amounted to 3–4 percent of GDP across the whole economy).[27] The alternative was to hide money from the tax inspectorate. Successful companies made every effort to avoid the appearance of making a profit. They set up a bewildering array of "shell-firms" that produced nothing but served as entrepôts for funds that were destined for hard currency bank accounts abroad before (sometimes) returning to Russia. These convoluted accounting procedures consistently made Cyprus one of the top five investors in the Russian economy, on a par with France and Britain.[28]

The same basic principles – to avoid recording money transactions and to make economic life as untransparent as possible – were also adopted by less profitable or internationally connected companies. In 1994, struggling to keep pace with the market, impoverished enterprises turned to barter in preference to cash transactions. This practice grew over the following couple of years, despite the stabilization of the currency. The result was a demonetization of the economy reminiscent of the Soviet era. By 1998, it was estimated that between 50 and 70 percent of sales in industry did not use the state-issued money.[29] Most Russian enterprises evaded public scrutiny by choosing not to trade on the stock market. Accounting procedures allowed them to blur the distinction between "real" cash and illiquid "virtual" rubles. Company accounts did not distinguish between money and other forms of income such as tax offsets, promissory notes, and goods received in barter transactions.[30]

If so many enterprises were exchanging goods and offsetting each other's debts in the absence of an adequate money supply, who exactly was making money in the Russian economy? The main revenue generators were the energy companies who produced oil and gas cheaply and sold them on robust international markets. In the first instance, that meant the gigantic corporation Gazprom, which had more than 350,000 employees, directly supported a further 6 million people, and accounted for about 8 percent of Russia's GDP.[31] Gazprom kept less profitable enterprises afloat by offering subsidized prices on the internal market and tolerating non-payment by Russian customers. Thanks to the lavish tax breaks it received from the state, it could afford this largess and still have plenty left to fill the hard currency bank accounts of its major stakeholders.

From the cash cows of the energy sector to the lame ducks of the rustbelt, all parts of the Russian economy participated to some extent in an economy where value was systematically concealed and where money was redistributed less through taxation than by various unofficial means. According to one informed estimate in early 2001, as much as 45 percent of goods and services in Russia was provided by the "shadow economy."[32] The opacity of Russian business practices led some economists to throw up their hands in exasperation and speak of a "virtual economy."[33] In one sense, therefore, there was strikingly little progress in the first ten years of economic transition. Just as money had little meaning in late Soviet Russia unless it was accompanied by the right contacts and access to resources, so large parts of the Russian economy in the late 1990s remained substantially demonetized. The state and the rule of law appeared chronically weak. The Russian apostles of the free market had shown that, when push came to shove, political power and tactical advantage were more of a priority for them than either freedom or markets – not to mention the well-being of the population. The transition to capitalism, apart from being partial, was crushingly unfair: it brought penury to tens of millions of people and the gross enrichment of a few tens of thousands.

The main argument in defense of the reforms as they were carried out is that, to adopt one of Margaret Thatcher's dicta, "there was no alternative." In 1991, the Russian government faced the challenge of changing the habits of a corrupt and decrepit, but enormous and supremely well-endowed, superpower economy. It had to face incessant conservative opposition from parliamentary politicians and vested interests in the system. Time was of the essence, and gradual measures – such as Gorbachev had attempted – would only have exacerbated a situation that was already a crisis. Drastic action was called for, even if it was bound to leave scope for abuses. According to this interpretation, post-Soviet Russia was no more than the past of American capitalism: this was the ugly phase of primary capital accumulation, attended by various gangsterish phenomena, after which the phase of regular market activity would ensue.

It would be nice to believe in this analogy, but it seems seriously flawed. The robber barons of the American past were not scavenging the assets of a collapsing, but enormously wealthy, ex-superpower. By comparison with Berezovsky, Khodorkovsky, and Abramovich, they were competing for small change. If we return to the reformers' non-falsifiable claim that alternative reform paths would have been worse, it seems legitimate, and necessary, to ask questions of the sequencing of reform. Was it right to privatize state enterprises at breakneck speed when they were bound to be snaffled by asset-strippers? Should the state have withdrawn from economic life with such haste without making more effort to ensure that there were enforceable ground rules in place to guide the activities of the new market actors? The first ten years of capitalism in post-communist Russia showed that there was no shortage of entrepreneurial energy in Russian society, but also that the legal and institutional framework for business activity was painfully inadequate. If an economy is to flourish and grow over anything other than the very short term, it needs the stability provided by the rule of law. But in Russia too many laws were poorly designed, contradictory, or unenforceable. As a result, the danger of a "partial reform equilibrium" was acute: by the start of the twenty-first century, most participants in the economy seemed trapped in a set of business practices that, while it offered profits or mere survival in the short term, blocked any prospect of long-term growth and improvement in living standards.[34] The economic "winners" of transition showed every sign of moving their funds to safe foreign havens instead of reinvesting them in Russia.

In short, the reformers were ultimately hoist by their own utilitarian petard. They were right to think that outcomes matter more than abstract principles and that people respond quickly to incentives. The problem was that they provided incentives for people to be crooks. Afflicted by a bad case of market hubris, they had a greatly inflated opinion of their own ability to direct the course of economic development and of the market's capacity, in the absence of a functioning state, to regulate human behavior. They maintained a doctrinaire insistence that politics and economics had nothing to do with each other – which, apart from being untrue, was belied by the logic of their own actions at times of political stress.

In the light of all this, it may sound odd to say that there are serious grounds to hope for improvements in the Russian economy. But a more optimistic case can indeed be made. This is not just to repeat the truism that Russia is a country rich in natural resources and human capital that is bound to prosper eventually. Natural resources can be a curse as much as a blessing, as they allow vested interests to turn a quick profit and to defer tough investment decisions. But oil and gas reserves, which are surely set to remain lucrative given the current global situation, will play a crucial role in Russia's economic consolidation if they buy the country a few years of relative stability. If people are behaving "badly" across a whole society – by evading taxes, concealing profits, abusing connections, ripping off shareholders, and so on – it is fruitless to condemn them or exhort them to behave like "civilized" Western capitalists. The only truly effective solution is to set up conditions where it will no longer be advantageous for them to behave in these ways. Stability and transparency are critical. If inflation is under control and standards of corporate governance are improved, perhaps ordinary Russians will start taking their money out from under their mattresses and investing it in banks. At about the same time, perhaps, banks will begin to accept that "regular" banking is preferable to quick profits on the currency exchanges: careful risk assessment and a system of finely calibrated loans will guarantee profits that are not so vulnerable to sudden downturns in state finances. It is possible, in other words, to believe in positive feedback loops and virtuous circles. The evidence is that people in Russia, as elsewhere, do change their behavior when the incentives are right. Most of them do not enjoy bending or breaking the rules: it is just that they have to. There is no need to demonize en masse the "Red" enterprise directors who conceal their profits and evade the short arm of the state. Some of them, to be sure, are corrupt and authoritarian, but others are simply trying all they know to keep themselves, and the workforce, and community for which they are responsible, in business.[35]

Perhaps the single greatest reason to look to Russia's economic future with expectation as well as with trepidation is the possibility that the state will reinvent itself as the referee of the market economy instead of a maverick player who likes to hog the ball. For most of the first post-Soviet decade, the state was so divided and dysfunctional that to refer to it by a singular noun does it too much credit. The Russian state of the 1990s cannot be seen as a unified actor trying (vainly) to impose order on a disorderly economy. Rather, it was made up of institutions and individuals whose interests were inextricably bound up – and sometimes simply identical – with those of the economic actors the state was meant to be policing. Ministers and *mafiozniki*, public servants and private vested interests, moved in the same circles. Gazprom, a company that remained substantially state-owned, was granted tax breaks that hugely benefited its private shareholders – one of whom, not entirely coincidentally, was Prime Minister Viktor Chernomyrdin. On a more local level and a smaller economic scale, state and criminal structures often struck up a symbiotic relationship. In St. Petersburg, purportedly "charitable" donations made by private businesses were found to have regional branches of the Ministry of Internal Affairs as their second largest beneficiaries. A significant proportion of the personnel in the private security firms that sold protection to businesses had formerly been employed in the state security apparatus. Of the 156,169 private security employees licensed as of July 1, 1998, about a third came from the Ministry of Internal Affairs, the KGB and its successors, or other security and law enforcement organizations.[36]

It would be easy to draw from these examples the conclusion that the Russian state is rotten to its core. A more sanguine, but perhaps also more judicious, conclusion would be that the state – as a law-upholding entity separate from society – is still emerging in post-Soviet Russia. In the first half of the 1990s it lost its shape entirely as its representatives lost the power and the will to gather revenue and maintain order. The Soviet state had been powerful in all kinds of ways, but its tools for maintaining economic order were limited to co-optation, coercion, and diktat. When the personnel system and command structure of the Soviet system disintegrated, the state had nothing to fall back on. Its habitual solutions to problems of economic malpractice – to appoint trusted cadres to investigate the matter, to punish the offenders, or to pass laws telling them not to offend – were ineffective. Time and again, state agencies were bested by informal networks and criminal structures.

There are, however, some reasons to believe that government in

Russia has emerged wiser and more effective from its chastening experiences of the 1990s: it has come to realize that capitalism is not incompatible with a strong state but rather depends on it. In Vadim Volkov's phrase, the state has for more than a decade been engaged in a "competition for the taxpayer" with other "violence-managing agencies" (otherwise known as "organized crime"): it was, in other words, "one private protection company among others" rather than "the source of public power."[37] With the right institution-building and legislative measures, perhaps the state can convince enough people that it would be safer and more rational to start playing by the rules; by offering a few carrots as well as sticks, it can perhaps induce the poachers of the post-Soviet economy to become game-keepers and good citizens.

The first term of the Putin administration gave some grounds to believe that these hypotheses are more than wish fulfillment. In the early years of the twenty-first century, the government did a significant amount to improve the transparency of the Russian economy. Legislative progress was made in a number of economically crucial domains: banking, taxation, land ownership, energy pricing, business regulation, and corporate governance. A much lower flat tax was introduced in order to encourage businesses to declare their profits more openly.[38]

But states are not just about setting the rules of the economic game; they are also about power. Almost fifteen years after the Chubais team announced their determination to get the politics out of economics, the future of the Russian economy still depends on political will. The early Putin era saw a crackdown on Mikhail Khodorkovsky, an oligarch whose company, Yukos, was one of the managerial success stories of the early twenty-first century. The charges against Khodorkovsky read like an account of the standard big business practices in which Yeltsin and his reformers had acquiesced for most of the 1990s. Yet, of all the tens of thousands of business people whose accounts would not have withstood the close scrutiny of the federal authorities, Yukos was singled out for treatment. Khodorkovsky was widely believed to have violated the terms of Putin's pact with the oligarchs: to keep out of politics in exchange for retaining the ill-gotten gains of the 1990s. He seems also to have brought down on himself the wrath of Putin by person-ally affronting a president who was slow to forgive or forget.

As the Yukos trial – which culminated at the end of May 2005 in a guilty verdict and a nine-year sentence for Khodorkovsky – abun-dantly demonstrates, Putin is not averse to using law in the same instrumental fashion as his Soviet predecessors: to treat the rule of law as a norm but also as a privilege that can be withdrawn from refractory or turpitudinous citizens. Although he believes in a strong legal system as the foundation of a strong market economy, his eco-nomic policy is never entirely divorced from his political objectives. At times this is no bad thing: his determination to build a strong support base in the rural areas that had hitherto been a communist stronghold led him to channel subsidies toward the much-neglected agricultural sector. But how far will political exigencies push him? In Russia's "virtual economy," the militarized rustbelt is far from being entirely a thing of the past. To transform it will inevitably require political confrontation; to restore it to something like its former position of prominence and privilege is also within the power of a president with enormous executive power.[39]

The Putin government has correctly identified the problem. The economy is too opaque and the law too weak for the market to be truly "free" (in the sense of offering reasonably fair chances to people according to their energy and ability). Through his "dicta-torship of law," Putin intends to force the market to be free. No one yet knows for sure whether this is a workable paradox or a self-defeating oxymoron. Only one thing is more or less certain. The Russian experience of recent years fundamentally calls into question the correlation that is often assumed between market reforms and democratization – between liberal economics and liberal politics. Russia's rulers have rated stability and economic growth a much higher priority than civil liberties – and a strong majority of the Rus-sian population has come to agree. In light of what most Russians have observed and experienced in the last fifteen years, can anyone really be surprised?

6 | Surviving post-socialism

As time passes, the people who fail to benefit from epoch-making events tend to slip from public view and memory – or to be branded reactionaries. Political change, in the language of social scientists, is notoriously "path dependent": new arrangements, often cobbled together in the heat of the moment, quickly come to seem self-evident, and the energy required to question and change them increases exponentially.

Forgetfulness with regard to the disempowered and maladapted settles like a deep fog over societies that have recently undergone massive revolutionary change. The sheer misery and dislocation attendant upon post-Soviet reforms were never given their due by advocates of capitalism – the "market Bolsheviks" – who were in too much of a hurry to think about compromise or equivocation. Yet the policies of these men quickly brought tens of millions of Russians into poverty and kept them there.

Demographic trends are the most striking index of the social costs of post-communism. The 2002 census revealed a population of 145.2 million, which was 1.8 million down on the last Soviet head-count in 1989. But this figure, which was boosted by net in-migration over the post-Soviet period, masked the true extent of the decline. A truer indication is given by the extent of fertility decline. The average number of children per woman plummeted between 1989 and 2002 from 1.83 to 1.25 in cities, and from 2.63 to 1.5 in rural areas.[1] Simultaneously, Russia saw an unprecedented peacetime decline in life expectancy. One economist's comparison of projected demographic growth with actual decline produced a figure of 3.4 million premature deaths caused by economic and social deprivation between 1990 and 1998.[2] The hard times of 1992–93 saw a marked increase in Russia's already high alcohol consumption. Largely as a consequence of this turn to the bottle, the Russian male population in 2025 is expected to be 7 percent lower than it would have been without the post-Soviet economic crisis.[3] Besides bringing general impoverishment and dislocation to the population, post-communism created numerous new categories of casualty: trafficked women, the homeless, refugees, AIDS victims, drug addicts. All in all, perhaps 60 percent of the Russian population could be considered "losers" of the transition, and a survey early in the Putin era suggested that only 25 percent of Russians could be said to have adapted "well" to the new conditions.[4]

However, while such sobering assessments have much value as a corrective to the gung-ho capitalism of the reformers, analytically they are a dead-end. To divide the whole of an enormous and complex society into two groups – winners and losers, or predators and victims – does no justice to the efforts of tens of millions of people who, in demanding circumstances, made strenuous efforts to get by, and even to prosper, as best they could. This schematic approach obscures the extent to which almost all Russians, not just those on the breadline, were in a sense "surviving": trying desperately to make sense of confusing economic and political signals and to find a way of operating in conditions of radical uncertainty. It also offers few insights into the direction of change and the likely outcomes of Russia's social transformation.

Any attempt to produce a more nuanced analysis of Russian society in the 1990s immediately runs into yet another problematic aspect of the socialist legacy: the fact that the language of social description had been cheapened, and to a large extent emptied of meaning, in the Soviet period. Back in 1936 Stalin had declared that the class conflict endemic in capitalist societies had been brought to a close in the USSR. Henceforth, the Soviet population would be divided up into three basic sections – peasants, workers, and intelligentsia – that would cooperate in the cause of socialist construction instead of engaging in destructive competition for collective resources. In reality, of course, the politics of class in the USSR was more about discrimination than about cooperation. The victims of discrimination were notably rural people, whose wages and pensions were miserably low; its beneficiaries were above all the party-state functionaries whose earnings were modest by Western standards but who enjoyed invaluable perks such as housing, holidays, and access to provisions not otherwise available in the shortage economy. Soviet sociology was always coy about the nature of the elite in socialist society, but such an elite surely existed.

An even greater obstacle to clarity, however, was the failure to make distinctions between the many different groups in the amorphous urban middle of Russian society. Clerical workers, doctors, teachers, professors, engineers, and managers were all lumped together, even though the prestige and life-chances attached to these professions varied significantly. One of the distinctive features of professional stratification in the USSR was that differences in prestige did not translate into large disparities in salary. A lot of the things that improved quality of life for Soviet citizens – family background, education, connections – were safely hidden from statistical inquiry and did not have an identifiable monetary value.

One thing, however, could be said with reasonable certainty. By the mid-1980s, Soviet society, like all societies that keep going for a reasonable amount of time in non-crisis conditions, had stable and widely understood unwritten rules. If an ambitious provincial wanted to be successful, he or she was well advised to seek a place in a prestigious university or institute in Moscow. Party membership was a good idea for those intent on pursuing an administrative career. If a person had the good fortune to be born into a reasonably well-educated family in a major city, all he or she needed to do was to complete a course of higher education to be guaranteed a respectable job that would in turn ensure a non-luxurious but secure existence. Even the less fortunate members of urban society could rely on a modest standard of living that their parents and grandparents had not enjoyed.

In sum, Soviet society circa 1985 was certainly not fair and equal – privilege was probably more hereditary than in many parts of Western Europe – but it was stable and less unequal than most non-socialist societies (largely, but not only, because it was also poorer). The standard of living was low by comparison with Western societies, and Soviet people complained – both in private and in public – about daily aggravations such as queues, bureaucracy, and overcrowded housing. But most of them accepted the inevitability of the existing order and saw that it had brought small but recognizable improvements over the past few decades. There is no convincing evidence that the Soviet population was radically discontented with its lot when Gorbachev came to power in 1985.

From 1987 onwards, the Soviet people were presented with enormously expanded opportunities to air grievances in public and to undertake critical reexamination of their economic system. At the same time, they saw the start of an alarming downturn in living standards and a collapse of the supply and distribution networks: by 1991, in many parts of the country, talk of starvation was more than scaremongering. Even worse, people entered a period of radical uncertainty that threw up numerous unanswered questions. Was the system of state redistribution gone for good? How much independent economic activity was it permissible to undertake? Was it wise to stick with a miserably paid job for life?

Some of these questions were answered by price liberalization at the start of 1992: this was clearly a decisive abandonment of the planned economy. But others reemerged with even greater urgency as inflation galloped onward. The most pressing question of all was simply one of how to survive on salaries and pensions that were being shredded by inflation.

Many Russians were undoubtedly forced to reassess quickly their notions of what constituted rewarding and prestigious employment. Not every official value in the Soviet period had been subject to erosion by popular cynicism. The ideological insistence on self-improvement and education struck a chord with a population eager to acquire the tools of modern civilization. Soviet people, even at the time I first encountered them in 1991, mostly accepted the socialist tenets that gainful employment, for both sexes, was both a right and an obligation, that physical labor had a special value and dignity (even if in practice people might seek ways to avoid it), and that income from many forms of commercial activity was "unearned" and illegitimate. This set of values could not, and did not, remain intact under the onslaught of primitive market relations. Education in institutions with a Soviet curriculum and rationale started to appear to many people at best a luxury they could not afford and at worst a waste of time. Likewise, the established Soviet hierarchy of professions was redrawn or even inverted. Fieldwork conducted in the provincial city of Kirov in 1994 (at a time when inflation was running to 20 percent per month) found that connection to economic activity was the common denominator in the list of occupations that citizens considered most prestigious: bank workers, lawyers, shop assistants in flourishing stores, directors of companies, and owners of private property. When asked to look back ten years and identify the corresponding list for the mid-1980s, they came up with a quite different selection: teacher, engineer, shop assistant, doctor, economist, lawyer, and the more highly skilled or senior industrial workers.[5]

To what extent did people act out these new commercial values? Small-scale business activity had taken off in the late 1980s, as new entrepreneurs got their start in the cooperative movement. "Entrepreneur," however, is a grand name to apply to many of these late Soviet businessmen, who were largely engaged in very unsophisticated buying and reselling. As a visitor to Yaroslavl in 1991, I was taken aback to find that several of the richest people I met were students of exactly my age, in their third or fourth year at university: they spent freely at the new commercial markets on food, drink, and consumer goods, and a few of them were even able to buy cars and flats. These young men made their money by exploiting the numerous deficiencies of the collapsing planned economy: they would acquire goods in one place and sell them down the road or up the train line. At that time, in cities like Yaroslavl across the Soviet Union, few organizations were taking upon themselves the elementary task of moving goods from the place they were produced to the places they were likely to be bought. Small groups of energetic, able-bodied, well-connected people were in a position to take advantage. They coordinated their activities and increased their turnovers by working through newly formed commodity exchanges (which, unlike their counterparts in the West, dealt not in stocks and shares and futures but in more tangible objects of exchange such as sugar, nails, and pots and pans).

The autumn and winter of 1991 were probably the high-water mark of such uncomplicated but profitable entrepreneurship. Small-time commercial operators benefited from the lack of competition (state institutions were still hampering the emergence of full-blown trading companies and still controlled, or blocked, the flow of many goods) and from the enormous but still largely unacknowledged devaluation of the ruble. After price liberalization in January 1992, the more ambitious entrepreneurs found that the big money was now to be made through currency transactions, by cutting deals with ex-Soviet enterprises, and by setting up large companies of their own (in which case they left much of the street trading and routine wheeler-dealing to their employees). If they were successful, they became enormously wealthy by Russian standards – and sometimes by world standards.

Lower down the economic food chain, however, there was a form of commercial activity to fit any budget (or any plastic bag). At the bottom of the scale, people might buy goods at wholesale markets or grow vegetables on their own plots and resell them at consumer markets or metro stations. Kiosks sprang up at all the nodal points of the city, offering usually modest income for their owners (who had to deal with both unfriendly bureaucracy and organized crime) along with low-paid and aggravating employment for their staff. "Shuttle traders" took cheap flights to Turkey and brought back cheap CD players and jewellery. Others did a roaring trade in pirated CDs, videos, and computer software. To take any kind of journey in Moscow in the mid-1990s was to be presented with dozens of examples of people "getting by" in the new commercial environment. Even the buskers, it seems, were not necessarily down-and-out victims but people making a rational decision about how to maximize their earning power. According to one informed witness of the time, an accordion player in the subway was able to earn the average Moscow wage.[6]

But a stroll through the teeming streets of the capital was also a misleading experience. Commerce was not an option that most Russians chose, or were able, to take. For one thing, opportunities of this kind were concentrated in large urban centers: Moscow, St. Petersburg, and moderately prosperous medium-sized cities like Yaroslavl offered enough consumers to keep a substantial commercial sector going, but the more remote and under-resourced regions did not. Another problem was that *biznes* was unattractive to many people. It was exhausting, time-consuming, and incompatible with family responsibilities. It was often stressful and physically dangerous. It still carried the Soviet-era stigma of "speculation" in the eyes of many Russians. It was also, quite simply, boring and depressing. Most people obtained a lot more satisfaction from their existing work: either because they enjoyed the content of the work itself or because of workplace sociability or (more likely) for some combination of the two. The dysfunctionality of the Soviet planned economy and the laxness of late Soviet work discipline had saved many Russian workers from turning into production-line automata. Soviet industry had seen relatively little deskilling and allowed considerable room for shop-floor initiative in meeting – or circumventing – the requirements of the central "plan" and the constraints of the shortage economy.[7]

Remaining at an ex-Soviet workplace also had the considerable material incentive that enterprises were usually the hub of provisioning networks. As much of the Russian economy moved over to hyperinflation and barter in 1991–92, it was better to be paid in groceries or consumer goods than in fast-depreciating or non-existent rubles. This factor, along with the sheer lack of viable alternative employment in many regions, goes a long way to explain why workers did not abandon their workplace, strike, or riot when they were not paid for months at a time in the mid-1990s. Their apparent passivity in the face of economic tribulations that would have brought social revolution in other places at other times was also conditioned by traditions of workplace paternalism that, if anything, were reinforced by the desperate uncertainty of the moment. When people did not have any idea what the next week or month would bring, it was reassuring and not irrational to take refuge in the "labor collective" and delegate key decisions upward. By 1995, even workers who held shares in their own enterprises tended to be hostile or ambivalent toward privatization; hundreds of thousands of them willingly signed over voting rights in shareholder meetings to their senior managers.[8] Managers and enterprise directors, for their part, continued to deliver at least the basics of the Soviet-era social contract: they tended to keep workers on the books even when hard-nosed economic rationality would have dictated redundancies.

Although real wages fell in the 1990s, the productivity of labor declined to an even greater extent, and in the circumstances employment rates were surprisingly high.[9] Workers had to put up with a certain amount of deskilling – foremen might become watchmen, weavers might become cleaners – and they had to be more flexible and versatile than in the Soviet era, when lathe operators could expect to maintain an intimate relationship with "their" machine over several decades.[10] They also quite often had to share jobs. But they were not exposed to the ruthless exigencies of an open labor market, and they did not for the most part have to face what they had been brought up to regard as the worst of all possible social misfortunes: unemployment. At the end of 1994, about 60 percent of Russian employees were expressing fear of losing their job (at a time when real unemployment was running at an acceptable 7 percent). This radical mismatch between feared and actual unemployment, inconceivable in stable market economies, meant that things were never quite as bad as people imagined, but it also put them in a very weak position for wage-bargaining.[11]

In rural areas, similarly, there were few signs of people fleeing the Soviet workplace. Private farms made little headway in the era of reforms. By July 1994, almost 280,000 of them had come into existence, but, despite government incentives such as tax breaks and low interest rates, genuine success stories were few: economic conditions were unstable, capital was hard to come by, and property rights were still insecure. Most rural people sought shelter from these problems by remaining in their old collective farms (now mostly renamed "joint stock companies"), which controlled 80 percent of agricultural land.[12]

In a society where little seemed secure, the workplace remained a fixed point for many Russians. But this did not change the fact that times were hard. Workers were losing crucial social benefits that had previously been attached to their place of employment: the trend was for enterprise kindergartens and healthcare facilities to be municipalized. They were also hit more directly in the pocket. Between 1991 and 1992, according to the figures of a group of economists broadly sympathetic to the reforms, real average wages were almost halved; in 1996 they were still more than 25 percent below their level in 1992. Worse still, cash-starved enterprises were simply not paying wages to workers who were living from one paycheck to the next. In 1996, according to official state figures, workers in the transport, agricultural, and industrial sectors had been underpaid to the tune of $4.5 billion. When employees did receive some form of payment from their enterprise, it was likely not to take the form of cash: it would come either in goods produced by the enterprise itself or in goods that managers had obtained through barter arrangements with other enterprises. Workers at dairy plants or bakeries or well-connected parts of the energy or military–industrial sectors were at least likely to be sent home at the end of the month with goods that were readily consumable or salable – but workers at one coffin factory found that their salary came in the shape of a wooden box.[13]

In this context, poverty rose to staggering new levels. Even if we rely on official definitions of the poverty line (which were always well below the population's own assessment), at least one-third of Russians were poor in 1992–93 (about three times the rate found in 1991). In 1992 the average wage exceeded the poverty line by a factor of three; by 1995 the ratio had fallen to 1:8. In 1999 the official poverty rate went above 38 percent of the population.[14] The same official figures revealed a level of inequality that would have been socially pathological if it had occurred in well-established capitalist countries and placed Russia firmly in the same camp as the Latin American "second world": the top 10 percent of the population earned about four times as much as the bottom 10 percent in 1990, but fifteen times as much in 1994 and thirteen times as much in 1996.[15]

The troubling and disorientating effects of poverty included not only its sudden increase or its sheer extent but also its distribution. Soviet Russia had always known social groups that were vulnerable to impoverishment. To a large extent these matched the equivalent groups in other societies: single mothers, families with a large number of dependants, old people left on their own without family support, villagers in underdeveloped regions. In the post-Soviet period these people remained poor, but they were joined in that category by the "new poor": people who had enjoyed a respectable status and standard of living in the late Soviet period but who now found themselves in underpaid and prospectless jobs. The life-chances even of well-educated professionals and skilled workers were now under serious attack. In 1993, 40 percent of the population below the poverty line was to be found in families with one or two children where both spouses worked.[16] Families that had been comfortably off until recently might be laid low by unexpected downturns in their income flow caused by illness, inflation, or simple non-payment of wages. Post-Soviet life presented people with imponderable choices between bad options and worse: the unlucky ones would quickly find their economic fortunes sliding out of control.

They could not expect much help from the state. In 1993–94, social benefits (taken as a proportion of GDP) were only about half of those in Russia's post-socialist fellows, Poland and Hungary. Not only that, the opacity of the labor market meant that social benefits, as well as being woefully inadequate in absolute terms, were extremely hard to target effectively. Compared with other countries boasting some kind of welfare state, poverty in Russia did not correlate well with types of occupation. To continue to offer blanket Soviet-style benefits (for housing, healthcare, and so on) was certain to subsidize millions of people who did not need this assistance, yet any more focused set of criteria risked excluding millions of people who were genuinely poor.[17] In the mid-1990s Russian policy-makers took the latter path: according to one economist, changes in government policies from 1994 onward caused at least 30 percent of the increase in poverty that occurred in these years.[18] Yet the new "marketized" charges were simply too high for many people to afford, and government agencies were pushed into clumsy corrective measures: toward the end of Putin's first term, about 40 percent of the population was entitled to subsidies on utilities and housing.[19]

Given all these complexities, how can we begin to identify the permanent – rather than transitional – losers of the post-Soviet era? Many of them came from the amorphous middle class of late Soviet Russia: the professionals and clerical and technical workers. Some of these people were among the most spectacular "winners" of the economic reforms – most famously of all, Boris Berezovsky, who was an applied mathematician at a research institute until he launched his business career in the *perestroika* era. Others, however, floundered. According to one 1993 survey, nearly 50 percent of the "mass intelligentsia" were poor.[20] Many of these people were betrayed by the headlong abandonment of one of the axioms of Soviet wage policy: that education always be rewarded. Young people completing school voted with their feet. In 1990, 30 percent of the school-leaving cohort entered tertiary education, but by 1993 that figure had fallen to just over 26 percent. The only comparable fall in the modern world occurred in China – but that was brought about by nothing less than a cultural revolution.[21]

Education was not the only Soviet-era hierarchical principle that was upturned. Another was age. The Soviet Union, iconoclastic and youth-affirming in its early days, had over time become a paternalistic and socially conservative place. In many workplaces, length of service correlated safely with earnings, status, and access to useful connections. As the Soviet economy failed to modernize, skills acquired on the job over many years remained valuable and secure from challenge by younger workers. Post-socialism transformed this state of affairs. Now older workers were likely to be among the first to face redundancy or demotion, and the average earnings of men who by Soviet (or Western) standards were in the prime of their professional life (between the ages of forty-five and fifty-five) did not much outstrip those of new arrivals on the labor market. The desperate need to make a living, and the uncertainty of economic conditions, removed from these men the incentive and the opportunity to acquire new skills in the second half of their working lives.[22]

Some things, however, never change. Russian women continued to be much the less valued sex on the labor market, though post-socialism led to a sharp further deterioration in their status and economic opportunities. The Soviet Union was remarkable in an international context for the high proportion of women in employment, and in post-Soviet times the great majority of women wanted, and needed, to work. But between 1991 and 1994 female income as a proportion of male income fell from more than 80 percent to around 60 percent.[23] Especially in the emerging private sector, women were becoming the slave laborers of the economy. They were considerably more afraid of unemployment than men, and they had much reason to be: in a decade of belt-tightening, they were generally seen as an expendable category of worker in the more commercially attuned sectors of the economy. More than anything else, however, they were seen as docile and exploitable. Women's representation in most branches of industry increased after 1991 – at just the moment that the economic clout and viability of sectors such as metallurgy went into steep decline.[24] Similarly, tertiary education was feminized at just the time that it lost its prestige: female enrollments remained stable in 1992–93 while enrollment overall significantly declined.[25]

Old people were another large group of people adversely affected by the economic crisis of the 1990s. Pensions halved in real terms between 1990 and 1999. In the mid-1990s, about one in ten pensioners received the minimum pension, which was always below the subsistence figure and sometimes less than half of it. Pensions were not only small, they were not paid on time. Delays in the mid-1990s were commonly anywhere from three to nine months. Pensioners were exceptionally vulnerable to sudden downturns in state finances: in the wake of August 1998, the *average* pension fell below the official subsistence line.[26]

Yet to generalize about Russian pensioners from their almost universally low pensions is a risky business. To be sure, old people were among the most disempowered and deprived members of Russian society. They accounted for some of the most heartrending stories of dislocation in the post-Soviet era. In the far northeastern city of Magadan, for example, a few hundred elderly people – some of them former inmates of the Gulag, the rest migrant workers to this gold-rich and well-resourced Soviet outpost – found themselves economically stranded by the collapse of Soviet infrastructure and the end of their own working lives. They had to survive on the same pension as everyone else in a region where the cost of food was several times higher than in European Russia.[27] Yet in less inhospitable regions pensioners might find themselves by no means at the bottom of the heap. Pensioners had the advantage of receiving at least some semi-regular cash payments from the state, which was more than most workers could count on in regions where non-payment of wages was routine and society was moving to a natural economy. In 1999, for example, "only" about 20 percent of people of pensionable age had incomes below the official subsistence minimum; the poverty rate for the population as a whole was even higher.[28] Also important was the social context in which old people operated. The word "pensioner" continued, as in the Soviet period, to carry quite positive connotations: as the retirement age was set low – sixty for men, fifty-five for women, and even earlier for both sexes in some branches of employment – many people could (and did) keep on working even after they started drawing their pension. They also had control of their property and were free of the most costly kind of dependants (young children), which often made them net donors to their adult children. One group of ethnographic observers have gone so far as to speak of pensioners in the economically "involuted" regions of post-Soviet Russia as a "labour aristocracy."[29]

Pensioners also had the advantage that there were a lot of them, and their numbers were set to increase as the population aged. In 2002, 32 million people were drawing a pension (not including invalidity pensioners), and the median age of the population had risen since the last census in 1989 by four years to 37.1.[30] These sheer numbers, combined with a well-developed sense of entitlement inherited from the Soviet period, made pensioners the only social group capable of civic protest on a scale to scare even the tough Putin administration. In January 2005, nationwide demonstrations against the monetization of social benefits threatened to bring the country to a standstill and inflict the first serious dent on the president's popularity.

The other factor that pensioners had in their favor was time to engage in the labor-intensive coping strategies essential for many people's well-being in post-Soviet Russia. In the major cities they could spend hours searching out the cheapest shop or market to buy butter or sugar. They took care of grandchildren while the harassed parents worked unsociable hours. And, perhaps most importantly, they threw themselves into the most widespread "survival strategy" of the times: they worked on garden plots. According to official figures in 2002, nearly 35 million Russian households had plots of land where they grew food, and only about half of these were in properly rural areas: the rest were cultivated by urbanites. And this was no idle recreational activity: household plots generated an estimated 56.5 percent of Russia's agricultural production on only 6.1 percent of the land.[31] Even the Magadan pensioners were able to find some kind of answer to their unspeakable predicament by growing their own vegetables on a raised spot within walking distance of the town that was dubbed "dacha hill" by the locals. The growing season was only twelve weeks, but it made the difference between life and death.[32]

The huge scale of the informal economy – more than 40 percent of the total in many sober assessments – has led some observers to conclude that perceptions of post-Soviet penury are greatly exaggerated. Not only do pensioners and millions of other people grow much of their own food, tens of millions of people are working "on the side" and engaging in transactions that never show up in economists' figures. Methods of calculating the extent of the informal economy are necessarily indirect and imprecise, but one assessment for 2003 concluded that the total number of man hours spent in the informal economy was 14 percent of the total time spent working (and in some sectors – for example, agriculture, wholesale trade, and repair workshops – the figure was considerably higher than that).[33] It was further estimated that large and medium companies concealed about 15–18 percent of their turnover, that small businesses concealed 30–33 percent, and that real wages were probably 50 percent higher than declared.[34]

Russians, then, may not live quite as badly as their pitiful salaries and pensions would seem to indicate. They can draw on hidden income and on non-monetary resources such as the trusty "social capital" of contacts and networks. They are also still shielded from some of the main costs of living in the West. Russian households, according to one recent estimate, allot only about 6 percent of their income to housing and utility payments (as compared with more than 20 percent in Poland and Hungary).[35] Perhaps, in fact, researchers are too prone to a "catastrophist" mindset that assumes universal impoverishment and ignores countervailing indicators such as increasing consumer expenditure.[36]

This kind of skepticism has much value. Figures on reported income in Russia are undoubtedly misleading; so are public opinion surveys, where many people overstate the extent of their hardship and understate income. To talk down the state of one's own finances is prudent both psychologically and pragmatically in a country where economic bubbles burst regularly and most people earn more than they would like the tax inspectorate to know about. Surveys where people make assessments of their own well-being usually reflect their general attitudes to reforms as much as they do people's real standard of living. The gap between reported income and observed household expenditure grew in the 1990s: something must have been making up the difference (and, given the weakness of the financial sector, it was certainly not bank loans). Millions of people have acquired high-quality consumer goods that in Soviet times would have required years of saving, luck, and good connections.

Perhaps, though, all this came at a price. As the market transition began, it was reasonable to hypothesize that the introduction of meaningful money into the economy would transform the character of human relations: that people would become more jealously protective of their time and their favors. It now appears, however, that Soviet-style social networks have not been torn apart but rather restructured. People now drink less, watch the clock more, and keep the monetary bottom line firmly in view – but they also need more than ever to work with people they can trust. The hiring policies of private companies frequently give preference to new workers who come to their notice through personal contacts. People already in employment continue to value open-ended social relationships that are very far from being obliterated in the post-Soviet workplace. Workers in private companies value above all family, wages, work sociability, good relations with co-workers and with immediate bosses. The major changes since Soviet times are that people now have more fear of losing their job, place less value on free time, and are more concerned about maintaining their own health.[37]

There is a danger, however, of idealizing social networks as a safety net against poverty, of imagining that, however bad the economy becomes, Russians will always be protected by a community spirit that has been lost in many parts of the capitalist West and by their doughty ability to find creative informal solutions to even the most intractable economic problems.

One major flaw in this analysis is the fact that impoverished Russians become and remain poor not because they lack bulging bank accounts – very few people have those – but because they lack the very social capital and other non-monetary assets on which well-being and monetary robustness depend. Most poor families could not grow their own vegetables, because they did not have their own plot of land. For one reason or another – perhaps because they had lost their job, or because caring responsibilities or illness had forced them to withdraw to the home, or because migration had deprived them of their old networks – their range of useful acquaintances had shrunk alarmingly. If they did receive assistance from members of the wider family, it was more likely to take the form of money rather than the services or connections that would have helped to put these people back on their feet. Under these conditions, the much-vaunted social capital could enter a precipitous downward spiral.[38]

Social capital was not every Russian's birthright: it was inherited inequitably from the Soviet period. The USSR was egalitarian in wage policy but inegalitarian in most other ways. When the unspectacular but respectable salaries that Soviet people drew were devalued in the early 1990s, their life-chances were substantially determined by their non-monetary inheritance: above all, connections and education. Parental membership of the Soviet Communist Party under the *ancien régime* continued to be a good predictor of young people's life-chances – not, of course, because such membership was advantageous on its own terms, but because it reflected a variety of social advantages that did not show up on any document.[39] The economic "winners" of transition tended to change jobs less frequently than the "losers," and they were more likely to continue in the profession for which they had trained.[40] Contrary to naive Western expectations, this was not an economy that rewarded entrepreneurial initiative: it favored disproportionately a few privileged sectors of the economy and incumbent elites within those sectors.[41] It is true that it increasingly offered incentives for skills and expertise: after the hiatus of the early 1990s, education regained its value for the emerging middle class. But access to prestigious education was substantially an inherited asset. All in all, Russian society showed distinct signs of settling back into a stable hierarchy. About 60 percent of society appeared to be located in the amorphous "middle" of low-paid employment; the remaining 40 percent was evenly split between an upper class well endowed with social capital and opportunities for self-betterment and a near-destitute lower class.[42]

Status divisions and hierarchies were nothing new to ex-Soviet people, but the social hierarchy had been greatly "stretched" in the post-communist era: the increase in social differentiation led to increases in people's perception of decline in their own circumstances. The new social order also allowed little scope for social mobility, reflecting a country that was crisscrossed by impermeable lines of disparity between regions and economic sectors. Muscovites enjoyed seven times the income levels of most other regions and a third or less of the unemployment rate elsewhere. They could marvel at consumer innovations – shiny Western-style supermarkets, Russia's first IKEA – that were remarkable in a country where nearly two-thirds of the population had been using ration cards to buy sugar as recently as July 1993.[43]

Much of the rest of Russia, however, resembled a patchwork of fiefdoms whose elites – governors, deputies, key enterprise directors – sought to batten down the economic hatches and safeguard the resource base of their own region. In these circumstances, the economic health of the region would depend largely on the lobbying power of this elite in Moscow. The delivery of pensions and other benefits was increasingly moved to the local level, where the size of social transfers depended partly on the resources available but even more on the size of the population claiming a particular benefit. In 1997, for example, over 150 types of social protection covering 236 categories of the population existed in Russia just at the federal level, and in total two-thirds of the population were entitled to welfare benefits. Almost none of this assistance was means-tested; much of it emerged chaotically, at several different administrative levels, in response to tight budget constraints and immediate social exigencies.[44]

In other words, there was far from being a level playing field across Russia in the distribution of resources and opportunities, and most people were stuck on the patch of turf where they happened to find themselves. Despite a brain drain that gave a brief boost to US immigration figures in 1992–93 and a wave of legal and illegal immigration from the "near abroad," the post-Soviet landscape shows more signs of localization than of globalization. Upping sticks was a difficult option for many Russians, largely because potential host regions tended to put up obstacles to non-affluent migrants (the worst offender was Moscow, which continued, in flagrant disregard of the constitution, to require a permit [*propiska*] for residence), but also because to move was willingly to relinquish precious social capital. Even the neglected pensioners in Magadan, presented with offers by the state to fly them west and rehouse them, preferred to stay put.[45] Intra- and inter-regional migration went down by a factor of more than 1.5 between 1992 and 2002.[46]

This meant that life in post-Soviet Russia became "de-modernized" as much as it became free-market and capitalist. Instead of taking their chances on an open labor market, people remained in jobs where the security offered by paternalist enterprise directors just about outweighed the inconvenience of not being paid. Relations between the elite and the bulk of the population became neo-feudal in some parts of the country, as "ordinary" people relied on discretionary benefits dispensed by governors and enterprise directors who had been turned into barons by privatization and decentralization. Outside a handful of major cities, barter and cash-free mutual aid became mainstays of the economy. Urban people everywhere took to the fields to grow their own food. In a bizarre reversal of conventional wisdom, the productivity of agricultural land improved as proximity to the city increased: given the number of urban or suburban people with no more profitable use for their time, the inadequacy of transport links to the agricultural regions of central Russia, and the complicated politics of property rights, "peri-urban" garden settlements were more viable than large private farms.[47]

Even if we move closer to the hubs of post-Soviet *kapitalizm*, many incongruous details can be spotted. Shoppers drawn into the new supermarkets by the magnetic pull of bright lights and spacious aisles were greeted by the rebarbative sight of armed guards at the door telling consumers brusquely to hand in their bags before entering the store. Outside the few Western-style emporia, service remained by and large sullen. Beyond the world of commerce, interactions with officialdom were rarely as routine and impersonal as

British or American citizens expect them to be: rules for obtaining a vehicle registration certificate or paying a road fine were usually opaque and subject to some form of negotiation "on the ground."

Many people have looked for signs of an emerging post-Soviet "middle class" as a crucial index of the progress of social and economic transformation. Yet even people who seemed to fit all relevant economic criteria behaved in ways antithetical to any known bourgeois ethos. Muscovite families with surplus income were not great savers: they spent freely on foreign travel, new kitchen appliances, and home improvements. But these bursts of expenditure were often preceded by periods of frugal accumulation of the necessary funds, and they were almost invariably accompanied by perceptions of hardship. Defunct Soviet-era washing machines or television sets would not be thrown out but moved to other parts of the flat, where they took on a new role as sideboards.[48]

All this should be taken not as evidence of a Russian proclivity to splurge but as a reasonable response to economic uncertainty. At a time when the currency was fluctuating and banks were anything but customer-friendly, the best thing to do with money was to turn it into tangible possessions. At times, therefore, post-Soviet consumer behavior was curiously reminiscent of the Soviet days of queues and shortages. People still bought goods "ahead of time": shoes for their children that were three sizes too big, boots for themselves for three winters hence. They still resorted to bulk-buying at times of stress: after the devaluation of August 1998, grocery stores in the major cities were once again stripped bare. But people did not part with their money uncritically. In fact, the avoidance of fraud was an obsession of post-Soviet consumers. I still vividly remember how the atmosphere at one low-key publishers' fair in the suburbs of Moscow in the mid-1990s was electrified by a lunchtime seminar on how to tell the difference between genuine and watered-down or otherwise adulterated vodka.[49]

The not unjustified perception of most people, even the relatively well-off, that life was risky and unpredictable made them unremittingly short-termist. Another defining characteristic of their day-to-day behavior was an unwillingness to work for the unspecified common good. In my twenty or so visits to Russia, I have been to only a handful of stairwells in apartment blocks that were not dark and unwelcoming and did not smell of rotting vegetables (and usually also urine). Yet the front doors of apartments facing on to those same stairwells have over the same period been transformed into reinforced steel barriers against the outside world. This order of priorities in large part represents a reaction against decades of enforced collectivism. But the problem also lies in the weakness of a mortgage market that might have begun to transform publicly maintained buildings into privately owned condominiums. While poorly targeted housing subsidies were maintained, people had no incentive to involve themselves in maintenance beyond their own front door.[50]

There is no doubt, then, that most people in post-Soviet Russia retreated to a domestic arena where income and expenditure, not politics or the common weal, were the prime concern. What is less clear is whether this is entirely a bad thing. In a 2003 multi-region survey of people's sense of well-being, 41 percent of respondents were not content, but determined to improve their situation; 30 percent accepted the current situation as an unavoidable stage of the reforms; only 4 percent declared themselves to be happy with their lot.[51] In a series of surveys conducted between 1994 and 2002, low incomes were consistently and overwhelmingly the greatest single concern expressed by respondents. Yet, from 1999 onward, signs of successful adaptation started to increase, especially among the young, and the rate of absolute hopelessness, along with the fear of unemployment, declined noticeably.[52]

What all this suggests is that the great majority of people are not drowning in a sea of post-socialist anomie but making strenuous practical attempts to adapt to conditions characterized by an uncertainty that it is hard for Europeans outside the former Soviet bloc fully to comprehend. More and more people have become employees in the private sector, where they tend to earn more, even though job satisfaction and career prospects rarely match their aspirations or their abilities: the troubled economy, combined with the glut of over-educated people, ensured that post-Soviet Russia was a hirers' labor market. The surliness of some post-Soviet service may be hard to distinguish from its Soviet antecedent, but I suspect that in many cases it has a different cause: the vivid sense of many of the people behind the counters that, given the abundance laid out before their eyes, life ought to hold out more promise for them than it currently does.

Even the reputedly inert and benighted Russian village has seen dramatic change. To be sure, the institutional structures of the collective farm were substantially retained in the form of agricultural joint-stock companies, but the balance of agricultural production has shifted decisively to the rural household plot. In 1991, state and collective farms accounted for 69 percent of output and households for 31 percent; by 2001 the large farms' share had fallen to just under 45 percent, while household output had risen to an extraordinary 51.5 percent of output. This spectacular increase had occurred in large part because rural people were gaining additional land by leasing or buying it on a private market that had emerged despite furious Duma opposition to the commercialization of land relations in the countryside.[53]

Nor is it really true that life in post-Soviet Russia has become a brutish war of all against all where trust has collapsed and people look out only for themselves. Many people – even some, both in the West and in Russia, who are no admirers of the Soviet system – are now inclined to sentimentalize Soviet life for the supposedly warm and disinterested quality of the human relations that sustained it. It is true that time in the USSR did *not* mean money, and that life could afford to be slower-moving and more open-ended than in the West. But life was also boring and frustrating for many people, routine tasks were time-consuming and exhausting, and people operated through mutual aid networks (known in Russian as *blat*) not because these gave them a warm fraternal glow of social solidarity but because they had to. In post-Soviet times, the informal exchange of favors has not by any means ceased, but its instrumental logic – the bottom line of quid pro quo – has come closer to the surface (in the city environment, at least). At the same time, the moral underpinnings of *blat*, in particular the role of personal trust, have not been swept away by the arrival of a version of capitalism. If anything, the role of trust has increased: in unstable times it is only prudent to cooperate with people of proven probity.

Admittedly, this version of trust does not meet the standards of social scientists looking for the emergence in Russia of a mature liberal democratic society. It is too exclusive: Russians deal readily with people they know, but are unwilling to extend generalized impersonal trust to strangers and institutions. But who, other than a simpleton, *would* trust the institutions of post-Soviet Russia? Here again we see a prudent response to uncertainty, not a sign of permanent social pathology. When Russians are given convincing evidence that formal structures work, they readily adopt them as a supplement to the informal sector. Let it not be forgotten that Westerners too often use informal contacts in preference to, or in tandem with, written rules: it is hard otherwise to explain why businessmen fly thousands of miles to have discussions that could equally well be conducted by telephone or video link, or why every minor contractual dispute does not end up in court.

Russian society is still far from believing that a new "normality" has been achieved in the post-Soviet era. But the sense of permanent crisis has begun to weaken. For this tentative perception to harden into anything near certainty, Russia will need at the very least a decade or two of high energy prices, responsible government and political stability. But, nearly fifteen years on from the start of Russia's socio-economic revolution, it seems legitimate to inquire whether any kind of new social order has been established.

Russia has certainly become a more unequal and divided society, and many of the inequalities and divisions seem irreversible. A few tens of thousands of people were able to enrich themselves on a scale and at a speed unprecedented in world history. Their money translated into power in all kinds of ways, and the prospects of 140 million of their fellow citizens now depend to a large extent on what they choose to do with this power. For the vast majority of Russians who have not made their fortunes yet, the quality of life is likely to be heavily determined by a number of factors: the region in which they live, their occupation, their level of education. These are "normal" conditioning factors in social stratification; what is abnormal in contemporary Russia is the steep inequalities to which they give rise.

The other decisive and disturbing social aspect of the Second

Russian Revolution is the fact that, like all revolutions, it let drop a historical guillotine on the population. The demographic continuum was severed into cohorts. Of all age groups, people in their thirties at the time of the Soviet collapse were most enthusiastic about the economic reforms and best placed to take advantage of them: they had education, social capital, and perhaps also living space from the Soviet period, but they also had the time and energy to adapt effectively to a transformed range of economic opportunities and pitfalls. People over forty-five, men especially, were in a bad way, as they faced an uncertainty and a social marginalization for which nothing could have prepared them. Tens of millions of people – almost entirely those in the older age groups – believed that their lives would have been better had the USSR remained in existence for another decade or two (which it might very well have done). They were almost certainly correct in this belief – and they were undoubtedly right in thinking that the hardship inevitable in so complex a transformation of so dysfunctional a system was greatly exacerbated by the policies of "liberal" elites who saw any scruple for popular welfare as a failure of nerve.

Russia's post-communist transformation, then, effectively pronounced sentence on broad swathes of the population: many were condemned to penury, a few let free to prosper. But this revolution, like many previous revolutions, may turn out in the long term to be fascinating not only for the dramatic ruptures that it brought about but also for the ways in which the present could never quite achieve escape velocity from the past. Most Russians have not prospered; but they have survived, and in the process they have worked furiously to bring their own experience and resources to bear on situations that would try the patience of a saint and the ingenuity of a code-breaker. Perhaps, in this light, it is time once and for all to declare obsolete the stereotypes of Russian passivity and inscrutability.

7 | Russia's war on terror

Terrorism is much more than a linguistic phenomenon, but it cannot escape being defined by language. As everyone knows, one person's terrorist is another's freedom fighter. Acts of terrorism in the modern world are accompanied by a less bloody but politically crucial struggle to set the terms in which such acts are described.

The semantic strife between perpetrators and victims, apologists and demonizers, rebels and the states they oppose, is fueled not only by the tactical and strategic considerations of the present but also by the pre-existing connotations of the word "terror" in a particular culture or society. Terrorism, for all that it raises absolute moral questions like no other political phenomenon, is not an ahistorical concept. It has multiple national histories in addition to the international dimension it manifestly occupies in the early twenty-first century.

Russia's historical experience of terror stands out as being exceptionally intense. Indeed, Russia has a strong claim to the dubious distinction of having invented terrorism as an instrument of modern politics. From the 1870s onward, certain groups of Russian revolutionaries publicly declared – and justified – their intention to kill in cold blood as a means of advancing their cause. The targets they considered legitimate included, in the first instance, members of the imperial family and holders of high political office, but by the early twentieth century the range of potential victims expanded to take in tsarist functionaries at practically all levels, both on and off duty. A recent scholarly estimate gives a figure of 17,000 casualties of terrorism during the reign of Russia's last tsar, Nicholas II. Political concessions did not necessarily bring a reduction of the violence: in the year following Nicholas's grudging acceptance of a parliament in October 1905, a total of 3,611 government officials from various parts of the empire were killed or wounded.[1]

The next stage in the history of Russian terror was for the revolutionary state to adopt violence as a systematic policy. In 1918 the Bolsheviks started to kill extra-judicially and in cold blood as a conscious political tactic. Moreover, they went much further than the earlier revolutionaries, both in the numbers they killed and in their willingness to kill civilians indiscriminately *pour encourager les autres*. Of course, their opponents in the Civil War were also not reluctant to shed non-combatant blood, but the Reds were much more explicit than the Whites in their use of terror as an instrument for achieving political objectives.

In the Soviet period, the meaning of terror changed once again. On the one hand, the purported enemies of the regime – such as the defendants at Stalinist show trials – were branded "terrorists" for the fantastic crimes to which they confessed. On the other hand, the state showed itself to be Russia's leading terrorist organization – notably by carrying out the arrest and execution of hundreds of thousands of people in what much later was publicly acknowledged as the "Terror" of 1937–38.

In the post-Stalin era, the state-sponsored violence of the earlier Soviet period was to some extent displaced in the popular consciousness by pride in the victory over Nazi Germany and a sense of relief that mass "repression" was no longer adopted as a technique of governance in the USSR. But state terror was brought back firmly to public attention by the rapidly proliferating revelations of the glasnost era. The Soviet population was suddenly granted an extraordinarily frank account of Stalin's crimes – and in due course of Lenin's too.

In 1991, then, "terror" in a Russian context meant violence perpetrated by powerful states against weak citizens. Russia exemplified a truth very rarely acknowledged in the contemporary Western world: over the last century, states – not terrorist organizations – have been by far the greatest perpetrators of terror. By 2001, however, the once-powerful Russian state was able with some plausibility to present itself as the victim rather than the perpetrator of terrorist attacks, and to push itself forward to the vanguard of George Bush's global "War on Terror." How did this remarkable turnaround occur?

The short answer to this question is "Chechnya." In December

1994 Russian troops crossed the border into this breakaway republic in the North Caucasus. On New Year's Eve columns of tanks were sent into the Chechen capital, Grozny, where they quickly found themselves caught up in a terrifying street battle. Hundreds of Russian troops were killed, while others fled in bewilderment and humiliation. The response of the Russian military command was to resume and intensify an air bombardment of the city that soon killed thousands of civilians. After that the violence did not stop.

What was the problem that called for such a drastic solution on the part of the Russian government and armed forces? Whatever it was, it emerged suddenly and unexpectedly for policy-makers in Moscow. In the federal structure of the RSFSR, "Chechnya" had not existed as an administrative unit: it was contained within the autonomous republic of Checheno-Ingushetia. In 1990–91 a power struggle took place between the "communist" establishment of the republic and a nationalist movement that gained its main platform in the new institution of the Chechen National Congress. This conflict, though on a much smaller scale, was analogous to the simultaneous standoff between Soviet and Russian institutions. And, in August 1991, it too was resolved in favor of the "national" cause. Chechnya became the first part of Russia itself to go the way of so many peripheral parts of the Soviet empire in Eastern Europe: it had a separatist revolution. A radical group in the Chechen National Congress, led by a former Soviet general named Jokhar Dudayev, took advantage of the political crisis caused by the failed coup in Moscow and overthrew the incumbent Party boss, Doku Zavgayev. Acting with Bolshevik decisiveness – this was a takeover that had more in common with Petrograd in October 1917 than with Prague in 1989 – the insurgents seized control of the key sources of political power in the republic: the television center, the radio station, the building of the Council of Ministers. They were able to draw on an ample supply of spontaneous and well-armed support as men streamed in from the villages and took possession of the streets of their capital. The still formidable Soviet security forces refrained from intervening, though relations between Moscow and Grozny became heavily strained by mid-October, as the signs of Chechen insubordination multiplied. The new leadership pressed ahead with presidential and parliamentary elections on October 27, which duly delivered a thumping victory for Dudayev – a result that was undoubtedly inflated by fraud and the sheer chaos of the electoral procedure, but one that reflected the predominant anti-Moscow mood of the moment. Having received his mandate, Dudayev wasted no time in declaring Chechnya an independent state. The response from Moscow, at the beginning of November, was a failed attempt to impose a state of emergency – which only boosted the political legitimacy of the hitherto little-known new president.

The Chechens' reasons for hostility to Russian overlordship were among the most compelling in the Soviet Union. Not only did they have a history of armed combat against Russian imperialism that stretched back, in both documentary record and popular memory, the best part of two centuries, they had also suffered one of the most sudden and decisive acts of ethnic cleansing committed by the Soviet state: between 23 and 29 February 1944, practically the entire Chechen population was herded on to cattle trucks and dispatched east. About three weeks later, they were thrown out on the freezing steppe of Northern Kazakhstan and left to fend for themselves. In one of the more poignant throwbacks of the Putin era, a few elderly Chechens were still seeking compensation from the Russian state more than sixty years after their deportation.[2]

Another reason that Chechnya was likely to pose acute problems for the post-Soviet state was that it was a closed and inaccessible society where many Soviet institutions had put down only shallow roots, and where corrupt local elites had generous room for maneuver. The "indigenous" (Chechen and Ingush) population, although by the 1980s it formed a substantial majority in the republic, had fewer educational and economic opportunities than the more urbanized and highly trained ethnic Russians. The Chechens' grassroots religious life – a version of Islam – had only been strengthened by the hostility of the Soviet state in the years since the Chechens had been permitted to return to their homeland in 1957. Chechnya also had a surplus of underemployed men and an arms-bearing culture characteristic of mountainous frontier zones in many parts of the world.

Yet, paradoxically, a large part of the causes of the Russo-Chechen conflict of the 1990s lay not in the various ways in which Chechnya might be considered remote, backward, and benighted but rather in the fact that it had been able to draw on Soviet resources and had been integrated into Soviet economic structures. Grozny had grown into an important center for the Soviet oil industry. It had a major higher education institution, the Petroleum Institute, which trained up two generations of technical experts and industrial managers. Despite its historical disadvantages, Checheno-Ingushetia was benefiting from a pan-Soviet expansion of educational opportunity in the 1950s and 1960s. By the Gorbachev era, some Chechens were overcoming deep institutional discrimination to make inroads in some of the most prestigious spheres of Soviet life: the senior ranks of the army and the upper echelons of the administrative and managerial elite. In 1989, for the first time, a Chechen, Doku Zavgayev, was made Party boss of Checheno-Ingushetia.

By 1991, then, Chechnya had a political elite-in-waiting: a largely secular, Soviet-reared military–technical intelligentsia. The outcomes of post-communist transformations depend to an overwhelming extent on the relationship between political elites and society at the moment that communism is overthrown. In Czechoslovakia, for example, largely thanks to the existence of a broadly based intelligentsia, there was enough common ground between leadership and society to keep liberal democracy on the rails despite the inevitable political and economic stresses of transformation: to ensure that the revolution remained more or less "velvet." In Chechnya, Soviet generals and oil barons were able to preside over post-communism in a republic where unconsummated hatred of Russian hegemony was easy to unleash and where unemployed young men and semi-criminalized groupings were on hand to provide the muscle. This was always going to be an iron fist revolution.

The new Chechen regime was good at mobilizing the population for gestures and acts of defiance toward the Russians, but it was much less effective at establishing a stable political system or at solving the numerous social and economic problems that afflicted the breakaway republic. Dudayev was an army man and a political novice: he had a taste for authoritarian solutions and inappropriate grand gestures (such as his offer of political asylum to Erich Honecker at a time when Chechnya had many more pressing concerns than the fate of fallen communist grandees). In his eagerness to take quasi-military control of the republic, Dudayev readily cut deals with local elites armed with Soviet weaponry; the Russian charge that Chechnya was a "mafia government" had much more than a grain of truth to it (even if Russia itself was far from invulnerable to such accusations). The population of Chechnya – both Chechens and the substantial but rapidly departing Slavic minority – had to endure lawlessness and collapsing public services. The plummeting legitimacy of the Dudayev regime was shown by the emergence of organized internal opposition – mass demonstrations in central Grozny and impeachment proceedings against the president initiated in parliament – which was brutally crushed in June 1993.

The issue of most decisive immediate significance, however, was Chechnya's relationship with Russia. Here the sources of conflict were legion. The two sides had to conduct hypersensitive negotiations over the distribution of the Soviet weapons located on Chechen territory: these were concluded in May 1992 by an uneasy agreement that probably bore only an approximate relation to the situation on the ground. In November 1992, Russian troops sent to the Caucasus to resolve a bloody dispute between Ingush and Ossets came perilously close to extending their campaign to Chechnya. Economic matters were another sore point. A Russian blockade gradually pushed Chechnya outside the federal budget, even though permeable borders and rampant corruption ensured that Chechen mafia groupings and warlords-in-the-making gained from these sanctions as much as other sections of the population lost.

The period 1991–94, then, was a time of antagonistic coexistence between Chechnya and Russia. Both sides abounded in hostility, greed, and brinkmanship, and they made little or no progress in resolving the fundamental issue that poisoned their relationship. By 1994, Chechnya was "not so much an independent country as a twilight zone, neither inside Russia nor outside it."[3]

Chechnya was unquestionably a substantial problem for the Russian government. Dudayev's declaration of independence challenged the territorial integrity of the Russian Federation at a historical moment when that state was desperately in need of consolidation.

His regime – a violent and corrupt dictatorship in a volatile region – constituted a threat both to geopolitical stability and to the security and well-being of the civilian population. By 1994, the epidemic of violent crime had spilled over the border: Chechens were responsible for a string of hijacking incidents in the North Caucasus. The stand-off with Chechnya was also an economic irritation. To the chagrin of Moscow's policy-makers, the most economically attractive pipeline route from the Caspian Sea to the West passed through Chechnya, and Dudayev was not slow to demand a cut on any commercial traffic passing through his domain.

There are so many ways in which the subsequent armed conflict can be explained that it is all the more important to remember that war between Russia and Chechnya was in no sense inevitable. Contrary to the claims made by Yeltsin and later by Putin, Chechnya was not about to trigger an avalanche of secessionist claims from other "subjects of the federation." Moscow still had time to adopt the strategy employed with other, albeit less militant, ethnically separatist regions: to offer the Chechens enough de facto sovereignty and economic leverage to keep them in the federation and, in time, to increase their degree of integration. Dudayev was an erratic and impulsive politician who was capable of unexpected statements of solidarity with Russia as well as inflammatory remarks. In the wake of Russia's constitutional crisis of October 1993, which brought the downfall of Dudayev's compatriot and ally-turned-enemy Ruslan Khasbulatov, there were some grounds to hope for a warming of relations between Dudayev and Yeltsin. However infuriating the experience might be, talking to Dudayev was still very much an option. Another option was simply to wait: the Dudayev regime, by 1994, was looking chronically weak as it lost touch with the largely criminalized groupings that controlled Chechnya's economy and arsenal.

But the most compelling reason why Russia's rulers did not have to go to war with Chechnya lay not in whatever hopes they might entertain of successful negotiations or of the natural wastage of the Dudayev regime but in their knowledge of what war in the Caucasus was likely to entail. Just as Russia had many reasons to wish for Dudayev's removal, it also had every reason to expect any armed conflict to be bloody, lengthy, and intractable. There were plenty of people in Moscow political circles who understood this. The problem, however, was that such people were sidelined in 1994 as Boris Yeltsin, his willpower fading and his patience with liberals wearing thin after the crisis of October 1993, moved hard-liners to the center of his political networks. A hasty, violent solution to the standoff in the Caucasus was duly adopted.

To begin with, Moscow's approach was not full-scale assault but rather the time-honored tactic for dealing with troublesome peripheries and Third World flashpoints alike: using internal opposition as a front for Great Power intervention. Above all, this meant funding and supplying with arms the "Provisional Council" of Amur Avturkhanov, a former policeman whose stronghold was the village of Znamenskoye in the north of Chechnya, close to the Russian border. Substantial military encounters between Dudayev forces and the opposition broke out in September 1994, with Yeltsin all the while insisting that this was an internal Chechen affair. By November, Avturkhanov and the other opposition leaders had made no progress, and the Russian hawks secretly committed their own troops to the fray in a tank assault on Grozny on November 26. The attack was a disastrous failure, and captured members of the tank crews were publicly exposed as being not Chechen oppositionists but rather bewildered conscripts who had until recently been stationed outside Moscow. Russia's military commanders accepted no responsibility for the escapade, but were goaded into compensatory reaction. The plan for invasion was thrashed out, with Yeltsin's approval and involvement, in the last days of November, and early in the morning of December 11 Russian tanks rolled over the border.

At the time, even before the human cost of the campaign became fully apparent, Yeltsin seemed to be paying a heavy political price for his decision. Contrary to hard-liners' expectation of a morale-boosting "small victorious war," the majority of the Russian population opposed armed intervention in 1994. The liberal mass media, which had tended in the past to back Yeltsin (sometimes against their better judgment) as the only reliable guarantee against communist revanche, now broke with him. By the start of 1996, Yeltsin's personal rating had fallen to single figures, largely as a result of the debacle in the Caucasus.

Thus, the first Chechen war, which lasted from December 1994 to August 1996 and ended in the recapture of Grozny by the Chechens and the effective defeat of the Russians, can hardly be considered a public relations success for the Russian government. Viewed at closer quarters, it looks even worse.

The conflict almost immediately departed from the script of Russian military planners. Their troops crossed the border into Chechnya with a publicly declared mission to overcome armed resistance quickly and professionally. Pavel Grachev, the Minister of Defense, notoriously boasted after the failed assault of November 26 that a single parachute regiment would have been enough to overcome the resistance in Grozny in a couple of hours. But the conduct of the campaign suggests that he thought otherwise. A heavy bombing campaign against Grozny started shortly after midnight on December 17. On New Year's Eve, after their firepower from the air had given Russian forces control over the approaches to the city, tanks were sent in with the mission to take Grozny within a few hours: given the feeble military resources the Chechens had at their disposal, this seemed realistic to military commanders. In the event, their assessment was soon made to seem criminally negligent. Although the Chechens had almost no tanks of their own, they were well able to deal with the Russians' military hardware: hand grenades and rocket launchers turned the Russian tanks into "moving coffins." The Russian commanders had committed the heinous error of sending tanks into battle without covering infantry. Worse still, they had thrown into combat young, inexperienced, and inadequately trained soldiers who were abandoned in the unimaginably terrifying conditions of street fighting in a city they did not know against an enemy they could not see.

The Russians' response to this disaster was to abandon all pretence of a "limited" war against a military enemy. They bombed Grozny incessantly and indiscriminately until Dudayev was forced to evacuate his presidential palace. Eventually, on March 7, they could claim to have taken the city – at a cost of thousands of civilian lives.[4] They continued with the same tactics as they worked their way through other Chechen rebel strongholds. The Russian army, with its immense firepower, was doing battle with an awkward and elusive enemy that increasingly resembled a guerrilla force. Given that the Yeltsin regime and the Russian army were not subject to the same accountability faced by governments in liberal democracies, they could permit themselves to inflict almost unlimited casualties on a local population that consisted entirely of citizens of the Russian Federation.

In addition, the Russian troops resorted to face-to-face terrorization of the civilian population in sweep operations (*zachistki*) and routine torture at the notorious and extra-legal "filtration camps." Many factors disposed the Russian armed forces to go far beyond the limits of "civilized" warfare at the first sign of trouble: the institutional brutality and corruption of the armed forces; their reliance on hardened mercenaries (*kontraktniki*) alongside conscripts; the breakdown of command structures; the inaccessibility of the terrain; and the neglect of the Moscow government.

The Chechens were facing an unscrupulous if dysfunctional former superpower, and they were inexorably pushed back. By the middle of 1995 their fighters had retreated to the hills, the Russians controlled the central plains of the republic, and the Chechen cause was hanging by a thread.

At this desperate moment, the Chechens entered a new, terroristic phase of their war with Russia. Its instigator, Shamil Basayev, had first come to public attention in November 1991 by hijacking a Russian plane to protest at the pressure being applied by Moscow on Chechnya. He then earned his military stripes by fighting in earlier post-Soviet wars in the Caucasus: in Nagorno-Karabakh and Abkhazia. By 1994 he was ready to throw himself into the struggle against Russia, and on June 14, 1995, a few weeks after Russian bombs had killed eleven of his relatives, he brought about the worst hostage crisis ever seen at that time. Together with 148 fellow fighters he smuggled himself 100 miles into Russian territory to the town of Budyonnovsk, where he wreaked havoc and held more than 1,000 hostages in a hospital. Although the Russians stormed the building, Basayev not only made it back to Chechnya with the help of a human shield, but also achieved his main political objective of a ceasefire in the war. Peace negotiations ensued, and an agreement was signed by both sides on July 31.

Budyonnovsk was a turning point both in the Russo-Chechen conflict and in Russian political culture. At a stroke, Basayev established himself as a successful and charismatic leader who was prepared to fight the Russians in a way very different from the tactics adopted by the two other leading figures, Dudayev and Aslan Maskhadov, who were both Soviet army men from the older generation born of postwar exile. His triumph came at a price, however. From now on the Russian authorities, whatever the blunders and abuses of human rights on their own side, would be able to paint the Chechens as terrorists with much greater public plausibility. Sure enough, in 1996, the Moscow media lost interest in embarrassing the government over Chechnya: their concern was to get Yeltsin reelected.

The ceasefire of July 1995 did not hold for long. The Yeltsin regime, conducting the negotiations with astounding bad faith, restarted its bombardment of Chechen villages; the Chechens fought back through guerrilla warfare. What reignited full-scale fighting, however, was Russia's attempt to install a puppet regime, headed by the same old Zavgayev who had been Chechnya's last Communist Party boss, toward the end of 1995. The final provocation was the decision to hold elections in December, before the full withdrawal of Russian troops. The separatists duly went on the attack, disrupting the elections and launching a full-blown assault on the town of Gudermes. January 1996 saw another appalling Chechen hostage raid, this time in the neighboring republic of Dagestan. In Chechnya itself the fighting resumed at full intensity.

The final phase of a war that ended well for the Chechens was initiated by the death of their president. In April 1996 Dudayev was killed in the foothills by a satellite-guided Russian rocket. Chechens went back on the offensive, and the Yeltsin regime – with one eye on the approaching presidential elections – restarted talks. The Russians once again proved themselves to be duplicitous negotiating partners, but a successful Chechen assault on Grozny at the beginning of August and the poor state of the Russian forces finally made a settlement possible.

What resulted was less peace than absence of war. The two sides had not resolved, but merely deferred, the crucial issue of Chechen independence. In January 1997, however, the prospects for stability started to improve. Internationally monitored elections were held in Chechnya, and Aslan Maskhadov was elected president by a solid majority. Like Dudayev, Maskhadov had spent most of his career in the Soviet army, but there were few other resemblances between the two men. Not given to rash outbursts and mood swings, Maskhadov was a man with some dignity and authority. By May 1997 he was stating publicly his intention to crack down on the criminal activities to which Dudayev had turned a blind eye. He also concluded an agreement with Russia on the crucial oil question. It seemed conceivable that Chechnya might in the medium term achieve substantial economic and political autonomy without offending Moscow's sensibilities or violating the constitutional arrangements of the Russian Federation.

None of this occurred, for reasons that were largely beyond Maskhadov's control. By 1996 Russia's treatment of Chechnya as merely a haven for bandits had become a self-fulfilling assessment. The republic's economy and infrastructure were devastated: perfect conditions for warlordism, corruption, and banditry. Kidnapping became one of Chechnya's main businesses alongside oil and gun-running; burning oil wells – set alight by owners who were not able to afford the necessary protection payments or hire their own private army – became a prime indicator of the state of the local economy.[5]

The pressure on Maskhadov came not only from criminal activity. He was also confronted with more articulate, if still armed, political opposition. Radicalized and islamicized by the war, a number of militant groups branded the new government a quisling regime for seeking compromises with Russia. One of their leading figures, Salman Raduyev, taunted Maskhadov for traveling to Mecca on a Russian passport.[6] Instead of Maskhadov's halting steps toward de facto independence within the federal structure, Raduyev and Basayev argued not only for an independent Chechnya but for a broader Islamic state in the North Caucasus. And they put forward their argument in deeds as well as in words. They were responsible for a series of terrorist acts – notably the kidnapping of foreigners and journalists – that could not have been better calculated to undermine the credibility of the Maskhadov government in the eyes of the wider world. Finally, in August 1999, Basayev launched an invasion of Dagestan that, although unsuccessful, left no doubt about his ambition to tear the North Caucasus away from the Russian Federation.

In September came a series of terrorist strikes against the Russian civilian population. More than 200 sleeping Muscovites were killed by bombs set in two apartment blocks to explode early in the morning; dozens more civilians died when bombs went off in the southern town of Volgodonsk and in Dagestan. Although the Chechen fighters never claimed responsibility for the Moscow bombings, and although six years later there are still intellectually respectable reasons to doubt their involvement, Vladimir Putin was able to launch a second war on Chechnya in 1999 with overwhelming popular backing.

This war proved even more physically and morally destructive for the Chechens than the first. Rather than uniting against the common enemy, they broke down into factions. Relations between the two main leaders of the first war, Maskhadov and Basayev, became fraught as the former found himself politically impotent and the latter permitted himself ever more reckless terrorist strikes. Against both of these men stood the pro-Moscow Chechen regime headed by Akhmad Kadyrov, a Sufi mufti who went over to the Russians in 1999 and became president in 2003.

Even this, however, makes the situation sound less complicated than it really was. The scale of corruption and devastation was such that the lines between the various political and military factions were not clearly drawn. For example, many former fighters had to be drafted in to staff the pro-Moscow president's police force. Clan and comradely loyalties cut across political divisions, and prominent Chechen leaders retained important contacts in the military and security services both elsewhere in the Caucasus and in the former Soviet Union more widely. The only certainty of life in the Caucasus was that all sides were vulnerable to violence. In May 2004, Kadyrov was blown up in a football stadium at a ceremony to mark Victory Day; away from the public eye, Maskhadov was found dead on March 8, 2005. Basayev continued to elude capture for reasons that were a matter of constant speculation: perhaps he was good at hiding, perhaps he had too many friends in the Russian security services, and perhaps the region's authorities were too corrupt to want to capture him.

Although the Putin regime claimed success in subduing the Chechen rebels as a recognized military force, the situation in Chechnya was disastrous for Russia too. This geopolitically hypersensitive part of the North Caucasus had been destroyed and brutalized, and there was little prospect of it recovering for the next generation or so. The situation looked certain to get worse before it got better: ten years ago, Chechnya stood out among its Caucasian neighbors for its militant separatism; by 2005, a similarly radical mood was taking over the younger generation in the formerly quiescent Dagestan, Ingushetia, and Kabardino-Balkaria. Nor was Russia's own younger generation spared: tens of thousands of Russian soldiers died in Chechnya (though many of them not at the hands of Chechen fighters), and the young men who did return were afflicted by a "Chechen syndrome" that made them unfit for civilian life.

The Russo-Chechen conflict, then, is a tragic story that must cast a dark shadow over any account of post-Soviet Russia. But its significance in Putin's Russia goes beyond even the human catastrophe it has brought to everyone involved. From 1999 onward, conflict in the Caucasus has been central to the way Russia sees itself and presents itself on the world stage.

Above all, Chechnya allowed the Russians to see themselves as crusaders against an international menace that the rest of the world had fundamentally misassessed. The atrocities of September 1999 enabled Vladimir Putin to brand Chechen rebels "terrorists," and that is how they have remained in the government-dominated public discourse ever since. Putin was also able to tap into a profound sense of national humiliation and resentment of the West. Such feelings came to a head over issues of national security. Russians felt themselves isolated as the European Union and NATO inched eastward. Opinion polls consistently showed that most Russians continued to regard NATO as a hostile organization. Anti-Western feeling, at least with respect to foreign policy, began to run high. The Russians' sense of abandonment was compounded when they started to fall victim to terrorist atrocities in the mid-1990s. Formal expressions of sympathy from Western governments and from the

UN were outweighed by Western disapproval of Russian actions in Chechnya, the separatist republic that provided the terrorists with their cause.

In July 1998, a new Law on Terrorism, the first of its kind in Russia, had provided a legal definition of terrorism and centralized the work of the security services, whose powers were expanded by further legislation in 1999. In December 1999, Boris Yeltsin, at the very end of his period in office, referred to Russian intervention in Chechnya as "part of the international community's effort against international terrorism," going on to warn the West that "international terrorism has no borders. It now has the whole world in its sights." In July 2000, Vladimir Putin, drawing on the rhetoric both of World War II and of anti-communist conspiracy theory, alluded to Chechnya as part of an "International Islamic Front" that was the work of "fascists" and a "terrorist international." For this reason, he declared, "Russia stands at the forefront of the struggle against this international terrorism. And Europe should get on its knees and show a large amount of gratitude for the fact that we struggle against it, so far, unfortunately, on our own."[7]

The events of September 2001 entrenched the terms of the public debate over Chechnya. Russians, with Putin at their head, observed 9/11 with horror but also with a bitter sense of vindication. They could claim to have been far more alert to the terrorist menace than their sleepy Western counterparts. The only difference between the assault on the Twin Towers and similar mass murders of civilians in Russian cities, or so they argued, was the televisual impact of the former. The Russian hand was strengthened further by the shocking hostage crisis in a Moscow theater in October 2002. Finally, in September 2004 in the North Ossetian town of Beslan, Russia was subjected to a terrorist attack so horrific and so excruciating when viewed on TV, that the rest of the world took note when President Putin proclaimed that Russia and the West were engaged in a common war against global terror.

Is this an accurate assessment of the situation? No one can responsibly argue that Basayev and his men (and women) are not terrorists in one commonly accepted sense of that term: they use extreme violence against non-military targets to spread fear in the civilian population, to gain publicity for their cause, and to put pressure on what they see as an enemy government to comply with their political demands. But to line up these Chechens alongside the putative wider forces of international terrorism is to make a further conceptual leap. Global terror, as conceived by statesmen and political commentators in the post-9/11 era, has a number of features that distinguish it from earlier forms of terrorism. First, it does not put forward a list of specific and notionally achievable political goals (such as national independence or prisoner release). Rather, it feeds off a more diffuse sense of hatred, resentment, or revenge. Second, it is carried out by people who lie completely outside the moral and rational boundaries of the civilized world. They may be the incarnation of pure evil, they may be religious fanatics, or some combination of the two. Proof of their hideously amoral nature is their willingness to target the most vulnerable and innocent of victims (not only non-combatants but also women, children, and people of their own religious or ethnic group) and also their readiness (even eagerness) to sacrifice their own lives. Third, this new strain of terrorism crosses national boundaries and relies on global networks to supply funding, expertise, inspiration, and other forms of support.

What this means is that governments can feel justified in adopting the most uncompromising counter-measures. As well as the traditional reason for not negotiating with terrorists ("we don't give in to blackmail") our leaders can point to the fact that modern terrorists often do not present a list of demands: they seem to relish destruction for its own sake. When we are confronted by such an opponent, they argue, we have no choice but to join battle.

How does the Chechen case match up to this notion of modern global terrorism? Vladimir Putin sees no difference between the two. In the speech he gave in the wake of Beslan, he did not even mention the word "Chechnya." The state media identified among the culprits nine "Arabs" and one "black" (*negr*). (This completely erroneous report was later retracted.) On September 3, in the midst of the Beslan crisis, the main evening news broadcast (Vremia) mentioned Maskhadov and Bin Laden in one breath and spoke vaguely of Islamic terror cells.[8] Maskhadov, the least extreme of all Chechen leaders since 1991, was later denied a decent burial by the Russian authorities under the stipulations of the terrorist law.[9]

Can it be said, following Putin and the Russian media, that the groups waging terror on Russia's civilian population since the mid-1990s had no identifiable political agenda more localized than the creation of a pan-Islamic empire of violence? If we look back as far as Budyonnovsk, it appears they did. On this occasion, the terrorists' goal was to keep alive the cause of Chechen independence in the face of a war that was threatening to destroy them. The turn to terror was a direct consequence of the war going badly. Over time, however, the political coherence of Chechnya-related terrorist actions has declined. Part of this is to do with Basayev, who has always preferred outrageous gestures and shock tactics to political consultation and maneuvering. It also has to do with the fracturing of political authority among the Chechens after 1997: Basayev was always willing to sanction or personally take part in murderous raids over the border, but he gained much more scope for such activities as the effective power of the notional president, Maskhadov, bled away. The other main factor contributing to the Chechens' loss of clear political purpose is the fact that Chechnya is in so desperate a state, and has so many competing and overlapping power groupings, that it is hard to see how anything approaching the life of a "normal" independent state could be established.

Another criterion for membership in a global terrorist axis is non-instrumental ideological fanaticism – which usually means the belief system of radical Islam with a strong admixture of anti-Westernism. Here again there has been some change over time. The two most prominent Chechen leaders before Basayev – Dudayev and Maskhadov – were secular products of the Soviet military system when they first became involved in Chechen politics. Dudayev's desire to build himself up as a national leader quickly drew him toward Islam as a means of bolstering his authority. But his religion was skin-deep: he learned far more about ethnic identity from observing the Estonian nationalist movement when stationed in Tartu in the late 1980s than he ever did from the Koran. In any case, indigenous Chechen Islam was a home-grown and parochial religious community that had little in common with the radical globalized Islam of al-Qaeda. In the course of the first war with post-Soviet Russia it would appear that the Chechen forces were swelled by no more than a few dozen fighters from the wider Islamic world.[10]

Chechnya did, however, become undeniably more nationalist in the early 1990s, and its national identity was a work in progress where the balance between kin, ethnic, political, and religious allegiances was constantly tilting. In the second half of the 1990s, Chechen political discourse became rapidly more islamicized. In large part this was a matter of generational turnover. The men who had been born in the early years of the exile of the Chechen people (in the late 1940s and early 1950s) and had made their early careers in Soviet institutions began to pass from the scene to be replaced by a radicalized younger cohort led by Basayev (b. 1965) who were eager to adopt the language, style, and tactics of the Islamic terrorism they saw on their TV screens. In 1994 the slogan most likely to be on the lips of the Chechen fighters was "Freedom or Death"; by 1997 it had been replaced by "Victory or Paradise."[11] But even among the younger generation religious ideology was not primary: young men turned to radical Islam because that had become the established idiom of violence, they did not turn to violence because they had been brainwashed by a particular version of Islam. As Thomas de Waal comments: "A radical fringe of the Chechens has become Islamicised without much foreign help at all. They have grafted what they have learned from Hamas and the Middle East – the paraphernalia of the suicide bomber, the videos, the belts strapped with explosives, the headbands and hoods – onto an older revenge culture and made themselves into very frightening creatures indeed."[12] In Chechnya, as in other parts of the world with a high incidence of violence against non-military targets, it is a misleading shorthand to say that terrorism is "religious": the forms and rhetoric may be religious, but causes and motivations mostly lie elsewhere.

The shift in the practice and ideology of Chechen terror is perhaps best illustrated by the history of suicide bombing. Until the late 1990s, non-military suicide missions were not part of the Chechen arsenal of violence. One of the perennial and highly valued skills of the Chechen fighter was the ability to avoid capture, to choose exactly the right moment, having inflicted the maximum amount of damage, to flee from an enemy vastly superior in numbers and firepower. When Basayev personally led his raid on Budyonnovsk, he had every intention of getting out of the hospital alive; and, against all the odds, he made it. By the time it came to the Dubrovka theater siege of October 2002, the Chechen fighters strapped explosives to themselves and took the role of *smertniki* (suicide bombers) as well as that of fighters. Over the following months the Chechens also launched a series of unambiguous suicide missions in crowded public places in the Caucasus. Many of these were carried out by women, which had the effect of increasing the fighting strength of the rebel cause without challenging the traditional male prerogative of fighter and survivor rather than self-detonator.

The final question to ask about the internationalization of terrorism in the Caucasus is the extent to which terrorist groups depend on outside assistance for organization and resources. This is a question that is bound to remain murky for the time being, and perhaps forever, but it is clear that funding, arms, and expertise have been provided from Saudi Arabia and elsewhere in the Arab world. In the second war, from 1999 onward, foreign jihadi fighters probably numbered around 200 out of total separatist forces that did not exceed 3,000. They were undoubtedly accompanied by some degree of financial backing from the Gulf (Russian security forces, who of course had an interest in overstating the degree of foreign support for the Chechens, named a figure of $6 million per month in 2000 alone).[13] We must remain skeptical, however, that these links make Basayev and others part of a global terrorist network in any meaningful sense. Chechen fighters have, from the beginning of the conflict with Russia, taken help from wherever they can get it. Often, that has meant taking bootlegged arms from Russia itself. In recent times, professions of radical Islam have bought Basayev money and manpower. Yet these gestures by no means make him an al-Qaeda operative. He shows no interest whatsoever in joining the struggle against the USA, the UK, and other states that stand accused by Osama bin Laden of aggression against the Islamic world. His published statements, whatever their pseudo-Koranic rhetoric, always return to a set of fairly concrete political demands: withdrawal of Russian troops, Chechen independence, the resignation of Vladimir Putin.[14]

Thus, although the Chechen rebel cause has become steadily more islamicized over the last ten years and has increasingly adopted terror tactics that are reminiscent of (though not identical to) those employed elsewhere in the world, the proximate cause of Chechen terrorist activities is not Islam or evil or global networks but rather war; or, more precisely, a particular war that was launched wrongly by the Russian state, and that has brought death and destruction and the elimination of even the remote possibility of the "order" that the Russian government claimed it had a mandate and a duty to restore in the breakaway republic. In the process, the Russian forces have carried out violent activities more sustained and destructive and no less undiscriminating than the many Chechen atrocities. In Anna Politkovskaya's trenchant phrase, the Chechen conflict was "state versus group terrorism."[15] Most close-quarters observers found the Russian soldiers at least as terrifying as the Chechen fighters – and far more terrifying in the sheer quantity of routine violence they were able to inflict on the population. Terror, indeed, came close to being a state-sanctioned tool of governance in Chechnya. Akhmad Kadyrov, the leader groomed by Moscow to take the reins of power after the second war, was remarkably candid in an interview of April 2002 about his ideas for restoring order in the region:

> To find a bandit, I would quietly gather information and appear at his door at two or three at night, shake his hand, and say hello. After such a visit, this bandit would disappear. With three or four other such operations, everyone would be clear on everything. That's just what happened when the NKVD was operating. One knock at the door, and the person would never be heard from again. People knew this and were afraid of it. That's how things were then, otherwise there would have been no order.[16]

The easy equivalence drawn in this passage between the Soviet police state and Chechnya in 2002 suggests that the most important conclusions to be drawn from Chechnya relate not to the North Caucasus or to any global "axis of evil" but to Russia itself. Over the last fifteen years Russia has struggled to establish a sense of nationhood or of political mobilization. By the late 1990s it was finally beginning to have some success. However, it gained a sense of unity less through positive achievements than through a common perception of crisis and conflict: by identifying enemies and by finding community in suffering. One of the clearest examples of this phenomenon came in Putin's speech to the nation after Beslan. The language was that of the War on Terror, but the rhetoric had more specifically Russian overtones. Putin declared that, although the Soviet system had not proved adequate to the challenges of a changing world, the Russian Federation was the Soviet Union's successor state. And, like the USSR, it faced colossal geopolitical threats. As Putin commented of Russian policy in the early post-Soviet years: "We showed weakness. And the weak get beaten up." Much the same message had been spelled out seventy years earlier by Stalin, who declared when launching his Great Break that the price of failure to overcome Russian backwardness would be catastrophic defeat in a coming European conflict. In other words, Putin was using the still powerful popular resonances of the Great Patriotic War to amplify his anti-terrorist message.[17]

Of course, Chechen atrocities gave him abundant rhetorical material. All terrorist violence tests a society's commitment to open, rational, and humane debate, and Russia has been more tested than most. In recent years, the incidence of suicide bombing in the North Caucasus has been higher than in Israel; in 2003 alone, Russia as a whole fell victim to more than 600 terrorist bombings.[18] If we take a longer historical view, moreover, it is hard to think of nations that have not relied heavily on war and conflict to hold themselves together in sensitive phases of development such as Russia is now experiencing. But, for all that Russia's current predicament is not without precedent, the case of a post-communist former superpower has its specificities: not least, the fact that it is sometimes impossibly hard to envisage where the conflict will end.

How do states pull out of the vicious spiral of violence and counter-violence that gives terrorism its momentum and a large part of its rationale? The only solution consistently proposed by the Russian state in the last ten years has been the comprehensive military defeat of terrorist forces. Not only does this method impose atrocious human costs, it also exacerbates the problem, or even creates problems where none existed. In 1991, the level of Islamic militancy in the Caucasus was vanishingly small; by 2005 it was substantial. The reasons for this change have much more to do with Moscow than with al-Qaeda.

The other main way in which terrorist conflict may be brought under control is through negotiation. The key question, however, is *how* exactly the parties are to be brought to the table. Occasionally, perhaps, there may be a happy spontaneous outbreak of statesmanlike behavior among key political actors. Usually, however, politicians need circumstances to prod them to the table. One factor that may dispose them to peaceful overtures is international pressure, but in the case of Russia that is unlikely to work. Western leaders never managed more than the mildest condemnatory noises during the critical phase of the mid-1990s, and in the post-9/11 world such noises have fallen away to a faint background hum. Even if the West were now to apply diplomatic pressure on the question of Chechnya, it would be too late and Russia would not listen. The War on Terror is the discursive successor to the Cold War on both sides of the former iron curtain, and to take advice from elsewhere would be to traduce a newly found sense of national purpose. It appears that unruly peripheries will continue, paradoxically, to constitute the vexed core of Russian identity.

The pressure to negotiate tends to be more successful when it comes from within. Terrorism usually occurs in modern democracies, because terrorists need public exposure. Even as the mass media condemn terrorist actions, they help to spread panic and a sense that conflict is not worth the human costs. The media usually also inhibit states from employing the most vigorous and indiscriminate anti-terrorist measures: as soon as governments are publicly perceived to have abandoned the moral high ground in their dealings with terrorists, they are in trouble.

By many of the key formal criteria, Russia now qualifies as a democracy. As a "managed" rather than a "liberal" democracy, however, it is not subject to the political mechanisms I have just described. The government has enough of the media under its thumb that it does not need to fear embarrassment. More importantly, even when political leaders are publicly exposed – and the lies and blunders of the post-Soviet era have been so palpable that not even the most talented spin doctor could hope to disguise them – retribution at the ballot box does not follow. It is not that the ordinary Russians are blind to the failings of their politicians: they are under remarkably few illusions. It is just that they do not quite have the priorities that we tend to believe citizens of European democracies "ought" to have. For the Russian electorate, "order" (*poriadok*) is a condition almost unimaginably more highly valued than in societies that have enjoyed stable prosperous liberal democracy for the entire living memories of the bulk of the population. Another problem is that Russian citizens, especially the great majority who are not affluent, have to struggle to imagine a place for themselves that is not a grimy corner of the Second World. Chechnya is an affront to their incipient sense of Russian nationhood, but it also speaks to their deepest fears and insecurities: as an impoverished, demoralized, violent, corrupt, and poorly governed nation-in-progress, Chechnya is not as unlike Russia as they would hope.

To the extent that Russians can form a satisfying picture of their nation, they must rely heavily, like Putin in his post-Beslan speech, on the tradition of statehood and great power status borne for most of the twentieth century, for better or for worse, by the Soviet Union. And here too there are profound sources of tension and ambiguity. To revert to the terms set at the start of this chapter, many Russians seek to bolster their resolve in the War on Terror by referring back to a state for which terror was a key tool of governance. The kidnappings carried out by Chechens in the deep south of Russia from 1994 onward were not the first such incidents in the area. In March 1921, the Bolshevik military command in the Kuban region authorized the seizure and incarceration of civilians as part of the struggle against Whites, Greens, and other opponents. Later that year, the order to shoot hostages came from Marshal Budyonny – the very same Budyonny after whom Budyonnovsk, the site of the key terrorist action of the first Chechen war of the 1990s, was named.[19]

Perhaps, then, the Chechen conflict of the 1990s was the revenge of Russia's past: in particular, of a twentieth century where violence was intense and largely state-sponsored, and where the distinction between victims and perpetrators was not always clear-cut. This is not to imply that violence is somehow imprinted in the Russian DNA.

A different biological metaphor seems more appropriate. Cultural and institutional antibodies to violence are not genetically inherent in human history: they build up over time, in mysterious ways, and largely through serendipity. Twentieth-century Russia, alas, saw plenty of unintended consequences, but little serendipity.

Afterword

It is hard to end a book on contemporary affairs without making at least a few predictions. In the Russian case, the most urgent task for a political forecaster is to assess whether the conflict and instability characteristic of much of the 1990s is likely to recur. From my present vantage point (January 2006) I would point to two main potential sources of instability. The first is economic: if world energy prices were to take even a moderate downturn, the Russian state might well find itself under intolerable strain. The second is political: the next presidential elections are scheduled for 2008, at which point Vladimir Putin will be constitutionally required to stand aside. If he does so, this would be an event without precedent in Russian history: a young, vigorous, and (perhaps) still popular leader would relinquish power without a fight. And even if all constitutional niceties are observed, the outcome of the elections might take Russia even further away from liberal democracy: Putin is by no means the most demagogic or authoritarian figure in contemporary Russian politics.

On balance, however, it seems prudent to avoid "catastrophist" interpretations of contemporary Russia. In the 1990s, to be sure, Russia underwent changes that can most adequately be characterized as revolutionary. Thankfully, many fewer people were killed than in France after 1789 or in Russia after 1917, but in other ways the transformation was just as radical. The Soviet state – whose coercive powers had in the past proved to be much greater than those of *ancien régime* France or tsarist Russia – was brought down, and entirely new principles of political representation and authority emerged to replace it. The boundaries of the once mighty state were redrawn, and tens of millions of people found themselves in countries they had never previously known. Economic liberalization tore up the fabric of everyday life, as ex-Soviet people could no longer count on prices, salaries, or even money itself.

Yet conditions of revolutionary uncertainty do not – cannot – last forever. Political conflict dies down, property and resources remain with their new owners, and new rules for economic and political life take shape. Among the population at large, sheer fatigue leads to a decline in political engagement; in the political elite, pragmatism and accommodation take over from incessant skirmishing. According to this interpretation, Putin is the consolidating "Thermidorean" leader who is announcing the return to a normality of sorts: patriotism, sober economic policy, rule of law at least some of the time.[1]

The great virtue of this approach is that it does justice to the magnitude of change since 1989 without making Russia pathological or placing it in a category of its own. We should not assume that, just because Russia has recently gone through very hard times and has patently not become a liberal democracy, it is a dictatorship predisposed to political extremism. The question we need to ask is not "Are the Russians becoming like us?" but rather "What *are* they becoming?"

Yet the "comparative revolutions" interpretation of recent Russian history also has potential shortcomings. It tends to subsume events since 1989 under the grand impersonal forces of history, leaving little room for individual agency or local specificity. It is easy to agree that Soviet Russia was not likely to move on from state socialism and the one-party system without political conflict. The previous order was in too many people's interests, and the social costs of economic liberalization were too great, for post-communist transformation to be achieved through consensus. But this is not to write off all the social, moral, and political costs of the 1990s as the collateral damage of history. The clash between president and parliament in 1993 may perhaps come to be seen as grimly overdetermined given the deadlock the two sides had reached. But the start of hostilities in Chechnya, which led to mass brutalization and tens of thousands of deaths, and the "loans for shares" deal, which signaled the Russian elite's contempt for democracy and legal procedure, were in no meaningful sense "historically inevitable."

An account of post-Soviet Russia can thus usefully distinguish between the good, the bad, and the unspeakable. What results from this more nuanced analysis is a conclusion that many Western observers, accustomed to imposing absolute categories on Eastern Europe, have found hard to swallow: Russia is neither a disaster nor a success story. It is not likely to become a fascist dictatorship or a geopolitical aggressor, but nor is it set fair for humane and prosperous democracy. The removal of the Soviet party-state was a great blessing, but the new regime of the early twenty-first century remains largely unaccountable to society – and thus more corrupt and unresponsive than European states west of Minsk. Russia is now in the grip of state-led patriotism, but at least it has not had civil war. The economic meltdowns of the 1990s, given robust energy prices, may not recur; but the very reliance on the ready cash provided by oil and gas will act against long-term development. The Russian population took heavy blows to its well-being in the 1990s, but has worked hard – though with varying success – to adapt to a new economic order that it now basically accepts.

In sum, Russia's destination seems rather less doubtful in 2005 than it did in 1989 or 1991. It matches neither the catastrophist prognoses of the 1990s nor the teleological scenarios of the transitologists. After a decade of precipitate change to arrive at the managed democracy and presidential capitalism of the Putin era, Russia may spend the next phase of its history going nowhere in particular.

Chronology

1989

February: withdrawal of last Soviet troops from Afghanistan

March: largely contested elections for Soviet Congress of People's Deputies

May–June: first session of Congress of People's Deputies

November: fall of Berlin wall

1990

March: elections for Russian Congress of People's Deputies

May: Boris Yeltsin elected chairman of Congress of People's Deputies

June: formation of Russian Communist Party

1991

January: Soviet forces attempt to suppress separatist movements in the Baltic republics

March: referendum on future of USSR and on creation of Russian presidency

June: Yeltsin elected president of Russia

August: attempted coup in Moscow; Mikhail Gorbachev resigns as general secretary of Soviet Communist Party

August–November: separatist takeover in Chechnya; declaration of independence by Jokhar Dudayev; failed attempt by Russian government to impose state of emergency

November: Yeltsin granted emergency powers for one year to carry out economic reforms

December: dissolution of USSR and creation of Commonwealth of Independent States

1992

January: liberalization of prices

October: Russian citizens issued with vouchers to buy shares; start of privatization campaign

1993

March: referendum on the conduct of economic reforms, the performance of the president, and the desirability of bringing forward elections

September–October: Yeltsin decrees dissolution of Congress of People's Deputies and Supreme Soviet; Supreme Soviet seeks to impeach Yeltsin; armed rising by Supreme Soviet is put down by force

December: election for State Duma and referendum on new constitution

1994

December: Russian forces invade Chechnya

1995

June: Budyonnovsk hostage crisis

November–December: "loans for shares" auctions of major gas and metals companies

December: elections for State Duma

1996

April: assassination of Dudayev

July: Yeltsin is reelected president of Russia

August: ceasefire in Chechnya

1998

August: Russian government defaults on debts and devalues currency

1999

March: start of NATO air strikes against Yugoslavia

September: bombs in Moscow apartment buildings kill more than 200 people; Russian forces invade Chechnya again

December: elections for State Duma; Yeltsin resigns as president; Vladimir Putin becomes acting successor

2000

March: Putin is elected president of Russia

May: Putin passes new laws to strengthen president's control over the regions

July: Putin announces radical tax reforms

August: sinking of the nuclear submarine *Kursk*

2001

January: introduction of flat income tax (13 percent)

June: new Law on Political Parties (imposes stricter conditions for party registration)

September–October: Russian government cooperates with USA over preparations for campaign in Afghanistan

2002

October: hostage crisis in Moscow theater

2003

March: US-led coalition starts the bombardment of Iraq; Putin describes the war as "a great political error"

October: arrest of the oligarch Mikhail Khodorkovsky on charges of fraud and tax evasion

December: elections for State Duma

2004

March: Putin is reelected president of Russia

September: Beslan hostage crisis; abolition of elections for regional governors

November: start of Ukraine's "Orange Revolution"

2005

May: Khodorkovsky sentenced to nine years in jail

October: rebels launch raid on Nalchik, capital of Kabardino-Balkaria

November: first ever celebration of "National Unity Day" (November 4)

December: Russian government announces tripling of gas price to Ukraine

Notes

Introduction

1 This line of argument can be extracted from several of the most ambitious synthesizing histories of Russia. See notably: R. Pipes, *Russia under the Old Regime* (London: Weidenfeld and Nicolson, 1974); G. Hosking, *Russia and the Russians: A History from Rus to the Russian Federation* (London: Belknap, 2001); M. Poe, *The Russian Moment in World History* (Princeton, NJ: Princeton University Press, 2003).

2 A. Ledeneva, *Unwritten Rules: How Russia Really Works* (London: Centre for European Reform, 2001).

1 What was Soviet socialism?

1 J. Kornai, *The Socialist System: The Political Economy of Communism* (Oxford: Clarendeon Press, 1992).

2 K. Jowitt, *New World Disorder: The Leninist Extinction* (Berkeley: University of California Press, 1992), p. 310.

2 The state: death and rebirth?

1 J. S. Migdal, *Strong Societies and Weak States: State–Society Relations and State Capabilities in the Third World* (Princeton, NJ: Princeton University Press, 1998).

2 A. M. Khazanov, "What Went Wrong? Post-Communist Transformations in Comparative Perspective," in Y. Brudny, J. Frankel, and S. Hoffman (eds), *Restructuring Post-Communist Russia* (Cambridge: Cambridge University Press, 2004), p. 32.

3 This account of the failures of the "First Russian Republic" draws on M. McFaul, *Russia's Unfinished Revolution: Political Change from Gorbachev to Putin* (Ithaca, NY: Cornell University Press, 2001), chapter 5.

4 The evidence of fraud – for example a suspicious mismatch between the number of votes recorded in the referendum and the number cast in the simultaneous Duma election – is reviewed in A. Wilson, *Virtual Politics: Faking Democracy in the Post-Soviet World* (New Haven, CT: Yale University Press, 2005), p. 75.

5 Iu. Shevchenko and G. Golosov, "Legislative Activism of Russian Duma Deputies, 1996–1999," *Europe-Asia Studies*, 53 (2001): 239–61; P. Chaisty and P. Schleiter, "Productive but Not Valued: The Russian State Duma, 1994–2001," *Europe-Asia Studies*, 54 (2002): 701–24.

6 K. M. Zisk, "Institutional Decline in the Russian Military: Exit, Voice,

and Corruption," in V. E. Bonnell and G. W. Breslauer (eds), *Russia in the New Century: Stability or Disorder?* (Boulder, CO: Westview Press, 2001), p. 80.

7 On Yeltsin's style of leadership, see G. W. Breslauer, *Gorbachev and Yeltsin as Leaders* (Cambridge: Cambridge University Press, 2002), esp. pp. 307–11.

8 See J. Kahn, *Federalism, Democratization, and the Rule of Law in Russia* (Oxford: Oxford University Press, 2002), chapter 5.

9 K. Stoner-Weiss, "The Russian Central State in Crisis: Center and Periphery in the Post-Soviet Era," in Z. Barany and R. G. Moser (eds), *Russian Politics: Challenges of Democratization* (Cambridge: Cambridge University Press, 2001), p. 121.

10 Kahn, *Federalism*, chapter 8; M. Hyde, "Putin's Federal Reforms and Their Implications for Presidential Power in Russia," *Europe-Asia Studies*, 53 (2001): 719–43.

11 Khazanov, "What Went Wrong?", p. 45.

3 Democratization?

1 J. Devlin, *The Rise of the Russian Democrats: The Causes and Consequences of the Elite Revolution* (Aldershot: Elgar, 1995), p. 54.

2 M. McFaul, *Russia's Unfinished Revolution: Political Change from Gorbachev to Putin* (Ithaca, NY: Cornell University Press, 2001), p. 79.

3 G. V. Golosov, *Political Parties in the Regions of Russia: Democracy Unclaimed* (Boulder, CO: Lynne Rienner, 2004), p. 25.

4 T. J. Colton, *Transitional Citizens: Voters and What Influences Them in the New Russia* (Cambridge, MA: Harvard University Press, 2000), p. 8.

5 Golosov, *Political Parties*, pp. 59–60, 64.

6 K. Stoner-Weiss, "The Russian Central State in Crisis: Center and Periphery in the Post-Soviet Era," in Z. Barany and R. G. Moser (eds), *Russian Politics: Challenges of Democratization* (Cambridge: Cambridge University Press, 2001), p. 125.

7 See Golosov, *Political Parties*.

8 Colton, *Transitional Citizens*, pp. 57, 60.

9 D. S. Mason and S. Sidorenko-Stephenson, "Public Opinion and the 1996 Elections in Russia: Nostalgic and Statist, Yet Pro-Market and Pro-Yeltsin," *Slavic Review*, 56 (1997): 698–717.

10 J. L. Gibson, "Social Networks, Civil Society, and the Prospects for Consolidating Russia's Democratic Transition," *American Journal of Political Science*, 45 (2001): 51–69.

11 P. C. Ordeshook, "Re-examining Russia: Institutions and Incentives," in A. Brown (ed.), *Contemporary Russian Politics: A Reader* (Oxford: Oxford University Press, 2001), esp. pp. 25–6.

12 Colton, *Transitional Citizens*, pp. 4–5.

13 T. J. Colton and M. McFaul, *Popular Choice and Managed Democracy:*

The Russian Elections of 1999 and 2000 (Washington, DC: Brookings Institution, 2003), pp. 27–8.

14 Ibid., pp. 19–21.

15 See R. Sakwa, "The 2003–2004 Russian Elections and Prospects for Democracy," *Europe-Asia Studies*, 57 (2005): 369–98.

16 Colton and McFaul, *Popular Choice*, p. 38.

17 D. S. Mason, "Attitudes Toward the Market and Political Participation in the Postcommunist States," *Slavic Review*, 54 (1995): 405.

18 Colton and McFaul, *Popular Choice*, pp. 18, 39, 220.

19 L. Gudkov and B. Dubin, "Institutsional'nye defitsity kak problema postsovetskogo obshchestva," *Monitoring obshchestvennogo mneniia*, 3/65 (2003): 39.

20 R. Rose and N. Munro, *Elections without Order: Russia's Challenge to Vladimir Putin* (Cambridge: Cambridge Univerity Press, 2002), p. 180.

21 Golosov, *Political Parties*, pp. 257–8, 267.

22 A. Wilson, *Virtual Politics: Faking Democracy in the Post-Soviet World* (New Haven, CT: Yale University Press, 2005).

4 Birth of a nation?

1 T. Martin, *The Affirmative Action Empire: Nations and Nationalism in the Soviet Union, 1923–1939* (Ithaca, NY: Cornell University Press, 2001).

2 Quoted in J. B. Dunlop, *The Rise of Russia and the Fall of the Soviet Empire* (Princeton, NJ: Princeton University Press, 1993), p. 58.

3 Quoted in ibid., p. 33.

4 V. Tolz, *Russia: Inventing the Nation* (London: Arnold, 2001), pp. 252–3.

5 E. Poppe and L. Hagendoorn, "Types of Identification among Russians in the 'Near Abroad,'" *Europe-Asia Studies*, 53 (2001): 57–71.

6 Dunlop, *The Rise of Russia*, p. 55.

7 Y. M. Brudny, *Reinventing Russia: Russian Nationalism and the Soviet State, 1953–1991* (Cambridge, MA: Harvard University Press, 1998), p. 259.

8 Tolz, *Russia*, p. 256.

9 G. Ziuganov, *Derzhava* (Moscow: Informpechat, 1994), p. 27.

10 A. Lebed', *Za derzhavu obidno …* (Moscow: Moskouskaia pravda, 1995), p. 448.

11 Iu. Levada, "Uroki 'atipichnoi' situatsii: popytka sotsiologicheskogo analiza," *Monitoring obshchestvennogo mneniia*, 3/65 (2003): 12.

12 M. K. Gorshkov and N. M. Davydova, "Istoricheskoe samosoznanie rossiian," *Monitoring obshchestvennogo mneniia*, 1/73 (2005): 17–24.

13 L. G. Byzov, "Zhdet li Rossiiu vsplesk russkogo natsizma?," *Monitoring obshchestvennogo mneniia*, 4/72 (2004): 22.

14 See for example "Troinaia diplomatiia Busha," *Nezavisimaia gazeta*, May 11, 2005, p. 1.

15 S. Rosenberg, "Russia Launches Patriotism Drive," <news.bbc.co.uk/1/hi/world/europe/4698027.stm>.

16 W. Zimmerman, "Survey Research and Russian Perspectives on NATO Expansion," *Post-Soviet Affairs*, 17 (2001): 235–61.

5 A free market?

1 A. Jones and W. Moskoff, *Ko-ops: The Rebirth of Entrepreneurship in the Soviet Union* (Bloomington: Indiana University Press, 1991), chapter 2; T. Gustafson, *Capitalism Russian-Style* (Cambridge: Cambridge University Press, 1999), p. 116.

2 A. Åslund, *How Russia Became a Market Economy* (Washington, DC: Brookings Institution, 1995), p. 42.

3 Dmitrii Rogozin, quoted in "Chego vy zhelaete Chubaisu?," *Kommersant-Vlast'*, June 13, 2005.

4 J. Bater, "Privatization in Moscow," *Geographical Review*, 84 (1994): 209, 211.

5 J. R. Blasi, M. Kroumova, and D. Kruse, *Kremlin Capitalism: The Privatization of the Russian Economy* (Ithaca, NY: ILR Press, 1997), p. 81.

6 Ibid., p. 2.

7 Ibid., p. 78.

8 J. Lloyd, *Rebirth of a Nation: An Anatomy of Russia* (London: Michael Joseph, 1998), p. 152.

9 Åslund, *How Russia Became a Market Economy*, p. 5.

10 C. Freeland, *Sale of the Century: The Inside Story of the Second Russian Revolution*, 2nd edn (London: Abacus, 2005), p. 14.

11 V. Volkov, *Violent Entrepreneurs: The Use of Force in the Making of Russian Capitalism* (Ithaca, NY: Cornell University Press, 2002), p. 2.

12 Freeland, *Sale of the Century*, pp. 38–9.

13 D. Hoffman, *The Oligarchs: Wealth and Power in the New Russia* (New York: Public Affairs, 2002), p. 315.

14 Gustafson, *Capitalism Russian-Style*, p. 63.

15 Ibid., p. 93.

16 A. Gnezditskaia, "'Unidentified Shareholders': The Impact of Oil Companies on the Banking Sector in Russia," *Europe-Asia Studies*, 57 (2005): 457–80.

17 Gustafson, *Capitalism Russian-Style*, p. 87.

18 Hoffman, *The Oligarchs*, pp. 218–24.

19 A. Guseva and A. Rona-Tas, "Uncertainty, Risk, and Trust: Russian and American Credit Card Markets Compared," *American Sociological Review*, 66 (2001): 638–9.

20 See P. Rutland and N. Kogan, "The Russian Mafia: Between Hype and Reality," in A. Brown (ed.), *Contemporary Russian Politics: A Reader* (Oxford: Oxford University Press, 2001), pp. 139–47.

21 F. Varese, *The Russian Mafia: Private Protection in a New Market Economy* (Oxford: Oxford University Press, 2001), esp. chapter 1.

22 Volkov, *Violent Entrepeneurs*, p. 34.

23 Åslund, *How Russia Became a Market Economy*, p. 138.

24 Varese, *The Russian Mafia*, p. 18.

25 C. G. Gaddy and B. W. Ickes, *Russia's Virtual Economy* (Washington, DC: Brookings Institution, 2002), p. 3.

26 Blasi et al., *Kremlin Capitalism*, p. 126.

27 Ibid., p. 130.

28 A. Ledeneva, *Unwritten Rules: How Russia Really Works* (London: Centre for European Reform, 2001).

29 D. Woodruff, *Money Unmade: Barter and the Fate of Russian Capitalism* (Ithaca, NY: Cornell University Press, 1999), p. 2.

30 W. Tompson, "Financial Backwardness in Contemporary Perspective: Prospects for the Development of Financial Intermediation in Russia," *Europe-Asia Studies*, 52 (2000): 617.

31 Freeland, *Sale of the Century*, pp. 71–2.

32 Ledeneva, *Unwritten Rules*, p. 2.

33 See, notably, Gaddy and Ickes, *Russia's Virtual Economy*.

34 J. S. Hellman, "Winners Take All: The Politics of Partial Reform in Postcommunist Transitions," *World Politics*, 50 (1998): 203–34.

35 For a case study that advances this argument, see K. Hendley, "Struggling to Survive: A Case Study of Adjustment at a Russian Enterprise," *Europe-Asia Studies*, 50 (1998): 91–119.

36 Volkov, *Violent Entrepreneurs*, pp. 169, 133.

37 Ibid., p. 26.

38 P. Hanson, "The Russian Economic Recovery: Do Four Years of Growth Tell Us that the Fundamentals have Changed?," *Europe-Asia Studies*, 55 (2003): 365–82.

39 S. Rosefielde, *Russia in the 21st Century: The Prodigal Superpower* (Cambridge: Cambridge University Press, 2005).

6 Surviving post-socialism

1 N. A. Zbarskaia, "Osnovnye tendentsii izmeneniia demograficheskoi i sotsial'noi struktury rossiiskogo obshchestva: Itogi vserossiiskoi perepisi naseleniia 2002 goda," *Voprosy statistiki*, 11 (2004): 63–8.

2 S. Rosefielde, "Premature Deaths: Russia's Radical Economic Transition in Soviet Perspective," *Europe-Asia Studies*, 53 (2001): 1159–76.

3 M. McKee, "Unraveling the Enigma of the Russian Mortality Crisis," *Population and Development Review*, 25 (1999): 361–6.

4 E. Avraamova and D. Loginov, "Adaptatsionnye resursy naseleniia: popytka kolichestvennoi otsenki," *Monitoring obshchestvennogo mneniia*, 3/59 (2002): 13–17.

5 J. Alexander, "Uncertain Conditions in the Russian Transition: The Popular Drive Towards Stability in a 'Stateless' Environment," *Europe-Asia Studies*, 50 (1998): 415–43.

6 J. Lloyd, *Rebirth of a Nation: An Anatomy of Russia* (London: Michael Joseph, 1998), pp. 212–13.

7 M. Burawoy, "The Soviet Descent into Capitalism," *American Journal of Sociology*, 102 (1997): 1430–44.

8 J. Debardeleben, "Attitudes towards Privatisation in Russia," *Europe-Asia Studies*, 51 (1999): 447–65; J. R. Blasi, M. Kroumova, and D. Kruse, *Kremlin Capitalism: The Privatization of the Russian Economy* (Ithaca, NY: Cornell University Press, 1997), p. 106.

9 V. Tikhomirov, "The Second Collapse of the Russian Economy: Myths and Realities of the Russian Reform," *Europe-Asia Studies*, 52 (2000): 207–36.

10 S. Clarke and I. Donova, "Internal Mobility and Labour Market Flexibility in Russia," *Europe-Asia Studies*, 51 (1999): 213–43.

11 V. Gimpel'son, R. Kapeliushnikov, and T. Ratnikova, "Veliki li glaza u strakha? Strakh bezrabotitsy i gibkost' zarabotnoi platy v Rossii," *Monitoring obshchestvennogo mneniia*, 4/66 (2003): 44–58.

12 L. Perrotta, "Divergent Responses to Land Reform and Agricultural Restructuring in the Russian Federation," in S. Bridger and F. Pine (eds), *Surviving Post-Socialism: Local Strategies and Regional Responses in Eastern Europe and the Former Soviet Union* (London: Routledge, 1998), pp. 148–69; G. Ioffe and T. Nefedova, "Russian Agriculture and Food Processing: Vertical Cooperation and Spatial Dynamics," *Europe-Asia Studies*, 53 (2001): 389–90.

13 Examples in this paragraph from Blasi et al., *Kremlin Capitalism*, pp. 108, 110, 111.

14 B. Silverman and M. Yanowitch, *New Rich, New Poor, New Russia: Winners and Losers on the Russian Road to Capitalism*, 2nd edn (Armonk, NY: N. E. Sharp, 2000), pp. 17–18, 156.

15 V. Shlapentokh, "Social Inequality in Post-communist Russia: The Attitudes of the Political Elite and the Masses (1991–1998)," *Europe-Asia Studies*, 51 (1999): 1172.

16 Silverman and Yanowitch, *New Rich, New Poor*, p. 50.

17 J. Braithwaite, C. Grootaert, and B. Milanovic, *Poverty and Social Assistance in Transition Countries* (Basingstoke: Macmillan, 2000).

18 K. Richter, "Government Cash Transfers, Household Consumption, and Poverty Alleviation – the Case of Russia," Centre for Economic Policy Research Discussion Papers, no. 2422 (2000).

19 A. A. Kolesnikova, "Oplata uslug ZhKKh naseleniem i sotsial'naia zashchita maloobespechennykh grazhdan v rossiiskikh regionakh," *Voprosy statistiki*, 2 (2004): 80.

20 Silverman and Yanowitch, *New Rich, New Poor*, p. 52.

21 T. P. Gerber, "Educational Stratification in Contemporary Russia:

Stability and Change in the Face of Economic and Institutional Crisis," *Sociology of Education*, 73 (2000): 224.

22 E. Brainerd, "Winners and Losers in Russia's Economic Transition," *American Economic Review*, 88 (1998): 1105, 1108.

23 Ibid., p. 1099.

24 S. Ashwin and E. Bowers, "Do Russian Women Want to Work?," in M. Buckley (ed.), *Post-Soviet Women: from the Baltic to Central Asia* (Cambridge: Cambridge University Press, 1997), pp. 21–37.

25 Gerber, "Educational Stratification," p. 236.

26 O. B. Oskolkova and O. V. Belokon', *Pozhiloe naselenie sovremennoi Rossii: situatsiia i perspektivy* (Moscow: INION, 1997); A. V. Pisarev, *Blagosostoianie pozhilogo naseleniia v sovremennoi Rossii* (Moscow: TsSP, 2001).

27 J. Round, "Marginalised for a Lifetime: The Everyday Experiences of Gulag Survivors in Post-Soviet Magadan," forthcoming in *Geografiska Annaler*, Series B, 87 (2006).

28 N. Tikhonova, "Social Exclusion in Russia," in N. Manning and N. Tikhonova (eds), *Poverty and Social Exclusion in the New Russia* (Aldershot: Ashgate, 2004), pp. 113–14.

29 M. Burawoy, P. Krotov, and T. Lytkina, "Domestic Involution: How Women Organize Survival in a North Russian City," in V. E. Bonnell and G. W. Breslauer (eds), *Russia in the New Century: Stability or Disorder?* (Boulder, CO: Westview Press, 2001), p. 244.

30 Zbarskaia, "Osnovnye tendentsii," p. 63.

31 V. M. Zherebin, O. A. Alekseeva, and N. A. Ermakova, "Lichnye podsobnye khoziaistva naseleniia: Sostoianie i perspektivy," *Voprosy statistiki*, 10 (2004): 56–7.

32 Round, "Marginalised for a Lifetime."

33 I. D. Masakova, "Sovremennaia praktika otsenki nenabliudaemoi ekonomiki i problemy po ee izmereniiu v usloviiakh modernizatsii natsional'nykh klassifikatorov," *Voprosy statistiki*, 10 (2004): 3–8.

34 L. B. Kuz'micheva, "Statisticheskaia otsenka ob"ema skrytoi i neformal'noi deiatel'nosti v torgovle v Rossii," *Voprosy statistiki*, 10 (2004): 13–15.

35 L. Skyner, "Rehousing and Refinancing Russia: Creating Access to Affordable Mortgaging," *Europe-Asia Studies*, 57 (2005): 561.

36 As argued in V. Voronkov, "The Corruption of Statistics," *Transitions*, 5/3 (1998): 40–5.

37 S. Clarke and V. Kabalina, "The New Private Sector in the Russian Labour Market," *Europe-Asia Studies*, 52 (2000): 7–32; A. L. Temnitskii, "Traditsii i innovatsii v trudovoi kul'ture rabochikh chastnykh predpriiatii postsovetskoi Rossii," *Monitoring obshchestvennogo mneniia*, 2170 (2004): 35–48; A. Ledeneva, *Russia's Economy of Favours: Blat, Networking and Informal Exchanges* (Cambridge: Cambridge University Press, 1998), p. 207 and elsewhere in chapter 6.

38 N. Davidova, "Poverty in Russia," in Manning and Tikhonova, *Poverty and Social Exclusion.*

39 Gerber, "Social Stratification."

40 M. Krasil'nikova, "Dinamika obshchestvennykh statusov za 20 let," *Monitoring obshchestvennogo mneniia*, 5/61 (2002): 33–9.

41 T. P. Gerber and M. Hout, "More Shock than Therapy: Market Transition, Employment, and Income in Russia, 1991–1995," *American Journal of Sociology*, 104 (1998): 1–50.

42 N. E. Tikhonova, *Faktory sotsial'noi stratifikatsii v usloviiakh perekhoda k rynochnoi ekonomike* (Moscow: Rossiikaia politicheskaia entsiklopediia, 1999).

43 V. G. Nikolaev, *Sovetskaia ochered' kak sreda obitaniia: Sotsiologicheskii analiz* (Moscow: INION, 2000), p. 92.

44 R. Kapeliouchnikov, "Russia's Social Safety Net: Standing at the Cross-Roads," paper delivered at NATO colloquium, June 1998, viewed at <www.nato.int/docu/colloq/1998/20-kapel.pdf>.

45 Round, "Marginalised for a Lifetime."

46 V. M. Moiseenko, "Snizhenie masshtabov vnutrennei migratsii naseleniia v Rossii: Opyt otsenki dinamiki po dannym tekushchego ucheta," *Voprosy statistiki*, 7 (2004): 47–56.

47 G. Ioffe et al., "Russia's Fragmented Space," in B. A. Ruble, J. Koehn, and N. E. Popson, *Fragmented Space in the Russian Federation* (Washington, DC: Woodrow Wilson Center Press, 2001), p. 75.

48 As observed by the ethnographer Olga Shevchenko in her "'Between the Holes': Emerging Identities and Hybrid Patterns of Consumption in Post-socialist Russia," *Europe-Asia Studies*, 54 (2002): 841–66.

49 The best method, apparently, is to look at the pattern of glue on the reverse of the label: if it lies in stripes, that means the bottle has come direct from a factory and has not been tampered with; if it is evenly spread, then the bottle must have been relabeled along the way.

50 Skyner, "Rehousing and Refinancing Russia."

51 V. N. Ivanov, "Sotsial'noe samochuvstvie rossiian," *Monitoring obshchestvennogo mneniia*, 1/69 (2004): 78.

52 N. Zorkaia, "Problemy povsednevnoi zhizni sem'i: Bednost' kak fokus vospriiatiia povsednevnykh problem," *Monitoring obshchestvennogo mneniia*, 1/63 (2003): 26–38.

53 D. J. O'Brien, S. K. Wegren, and V. V. Patsiorkovski, "Contemporary Rural Responses to Reform from Above," *Russian Review*, 63 (2004): 256–76.

7 Russia's war on terror

1 A. Geifman, *Thou Shalt Kill: Revolutionary Terrorism in Russia, 1894–1917* (Princeton, NJ: Princeton University Press, 1993), pp. 20–1.

2 A. Abumuslimova, "Chechens Fight for Compensation," *Caucasus Reporting Service* (hereafter *CRS*), Institute for War and Peace Reporting (<www.iwpr.net>), no. 275, February 24, 2005.

3 C. Gall and T. de Waal, *Chechnya: A Small Victorious War* (London: Pan, 1997), p. 106.

4 As always, the exact casualty figures are a matter of dispute. The estimate of 27,000 published by Memorial, the Russian human rights organization, seems too high. Anatol Lieven (*Chechnya: Tombstone of Russian Power*, New Haven, CT: Yale University Press, 1998, p. 108) gives 5,000 as the maximum number of civilians killed by the end of January 1995. What is not in doubt, however, is the traumatizing and brutalizing effect of the bombardment.

5 As explained in A. Politkovskaya, *A Small Corner of Hell: Dispatches from Chechnya* (Chicago, IL: University of Chicago Press, 2003), pp. 169–70.

6 M. Evangelista, *The Chechen Wars: Will Russia Go the Way of the Soviet Union?* (Washington, DC: Brookings Institution, 2002), p. 51.

7 M. A. Smith, "Russian Perspectives on Terrorism," Conflict Studies Research Centre, briefing paper no. C110, January 2004.

8 S. C. Hutchings, "Russia's 9/11: Beslan, Nation Building and Television's Representation of Terror," paper presented at BASEES conference, Cambridge, April 2005.

9 U. Dudayev, "Fight Over Maskhadov Burial," *CRS*, no. 278, March 16, 2005.

10 As estimated from personal observations by Anatol Lieven in *Chechnya: Tombstone of Russian Power*, p. 84.

11 U. Dudayev, "Chechnya: Ten Years of Violence," *CRS*, no. 265, December 8, 2004.

12 T. de Waal, "Comment: A War of Unintended Consequences," *CRS*, no. 265, December 8, 2004.

13 J. Wilhelmsen, "Between a Rock and a Hard Place: The Islamisation of the Chechen Separatist Movement," *Europe-Asia Studies*, 57 (2005): 44–5.

14 See notably Basayev's statement after Beslan: <www.kavkazcenter.com/russ/article.php?id=25985>.

15 Politkovskaya, *A Small Corner of Hell*, p. 27.

16 Ibid., p. 142.

17 V. Putin, "Obrashchenie k natsii," viewed at <www.polit.ru/dossie/2004/09/04/putin.html> (September 5, 2004).

18 M. Kramer, "Guerrilla Warfare, Counterinsurgency and Terrorism in the North Caucasus: The Military Dimension of the Russian–Chechen Conflict," *Europe-Asia Studies*, 57 (2005): 216, 247.

19 A. A. Cherkasov, "Institut zalozhnichestva na Kubani i Chernomor'e v 1920–1922 gg.," *Voprosy istorii*, 10 (2004): 106–13. Thanks to Erik Landis for this reference.

Afterword

1 An interesting full-blown attempt to place the fall of Communism alongside the other major revolutions of world history is I. V. Starodubrovskaia and V. A. Mau, *Velikie revoliutsii: Ot Kromvelia do Putina* (Moscow: Vargrius, 2001).

Guide to further reading

The following selection is limited to a few works in English that will provide much of the detail missing in this book and give some idea of the main areas of debate on the post-Soviet era.

Good general works include Stephen Kotkin, *Armageddon Averted: The Soviet Collapse, 1970–2000* (2001), which is short and incisive, and Robert Service, *Russia: Experiment with a People* (2002), which is fuller and less argumentative. Victoria E. Bonnell and George W. Breslauer (eds), *Russia in the New Century: Stability or Disorder?* (2001) is a useful and varied collection of essays. Even better is Archie Brown (ed.), *Contemporary Russian Politics: A Reader* (2001), which has nearly 600 pages of expertly selected material.

One of the many compelling aspects of post-Soviet Russia is the extent to which experts differ in their assessments of it. For a small sample of the spectrum of opinion, see the following works (whose titles alone should give some sense of the broad areas of disagreement): Peter Reddaway and Dmitri Glinski, *The Tragedy of Russia's Reforms: Market Bolshevism Against Democracy* (2001); Andrei Shleifer, *A Normal Country: Russia after Communism* (2005); Allen C. Lynch, *How Russia is Not Ruled: Reflections on Russian Political Development* (2005); Steven Rosefielde, *Russia in the 21st Century: The Prodigal Superpower* (2005).

Some very fine journalists have written books on post-communist Russia. For excellent, wide-ranging and analytical accounts, see John Lloyd, *Rebirth of a Nation: An Anatomy of Russia* (1998), and Andrew Jack, *Inside Putin's Russia* (revised edition, 2005). A tour de force of reportage is Andrew Meier, *Black Earth: Russia after the Fall* (2003). A masterful exposé of the economic shenanigans of the 1990s is David E. Hoffman, *The Oligarchs: Wealth and Power in the New Russia* (2002).

More specialized, but still accessible, studies of Russian politics include the following: George W. Breslauer, *Gorbachev and Yeltsin as Leaders* (2002); Michael McFaul, *Russia's Unfinished Revolution: Political Change from Gorbachev to Putin* (2001); Richard Rose and Neil Munro, *Elections without Order: Russia's Challenge to Vladimir Putin* (2002); and Stephen White, *Russia's New Politics: The Management of a Postcommunist Society* (2000).

The topic of Russian nationalism has been well served in recent years. Note especially Yitzhak Brudny, *Reinventing Russia: Russian Nationalism and the Soviet State, 1953–1991* (1998); John B. Dunlop, *The Rise of Russia and the Fall of the Soviet Empire* (1993); Vera Tolz, *Russia: Inventing the Nation* (2001); and Geoffrey Hosking's forthcoming *Rulers or Victims? The Russians in the Soviet Union.*

On economics, the books by authors involved in making policy in the 1990s are well worth reading. These include Anders Åslund, *How Russia Became a Market Economy* (1995), and later books; J. R. Blasi, M. Kroumova, and D. Kruse, *Kremlin Capitalism: The Privatization of the Russian Economy* (1997); and the various writings of Andrei Shleifer. For complementary, and often conflicting, interpretations of the economic transformation, see Clifford G. Gaddy and Barry W. Ickes, *Russia's Virtual Economy* (2002); Thane Gustafson, *Capitalism Russian-Style* (1999); Federico Varese, *The Russian Mafia: Private Protection in a New Market Economy* (2001); Vadim Volkov, *Violent Entrepreneurs: The Use of Force in the Making of Russian Capitalism* (2002); David Woodruff, *Money Unmade: Barter and the Fate of Russian Capitalism* (1999).

Post-socialist changes in everyday life are expertly explored in the following volumes: Sue Bridger and Frances Pine (eds), *Surviving Post-Socialism: Local Strategies and Regional Response in Eastern Europe and the Former Soviet Union* (1997); Michael Burawoy and Katherine Verdery (eds), *Uncertain Transition: Ethnographies of Change in the Postsocialist World* (1999); Caroline Humphrey, *The Unmaking of Soviet Life: Everyday Economies after Socialism* (2002); Alena Ledeneva, *Russia's Economy of Favours: Blat, Networking, and Informal Exchange* (1998).

On Chechnya and terrorism, see above all: Carlotta Gall and Thomas de Waal, *Chechnya: A Small Victorious War* (1997); Anatol Lieven, *Chechnya: Tombstone of Russian Power* (1998); and Matthew

Evangelista, *The Chechen Wars: Will Russia Go the Way of the Soviet Union?* (2002). Anglophone readers can now also consult the important work of a Russian ethnographer and former minister of nationalities who argues powerfully against any Western tendency to romanticize the Chechens: see Valery Tishkov, *Chechnya: Life in a War-Torn Society* (2004).

Index